Welcom

We're So Glad You Happened To Drop In!

Between these covers you will discover a gathering of recipes that represent the much-talked-about, highly praised, excitingly new bill of fare of The Cheese Factory Restaurant in Wisconsin Dells, Wisconsin. Our restaurant has been happily described as an inexpensive gourmet vegetarian eatery with excitingly delicious variations of meatless menus that for many patrons is, at first encounter, a brand new dining experience.

Indeed, with some of these recipes you, as chef and baker, may well be offering your friends and family their first encounter with cookery of this nature.

We are determined that you will be pleased and happy. All of these recipes have been tried and tested by the finest international chefs anywhere. We promise you will be:

Healthy with a renewed physical vitality through the universally acknowledged nutritional benefits of these offerings.

Wealthy in new innovative ideas that are sure to please the guests at your dinner table.

Wise in the knowledge of simple economic elegance.

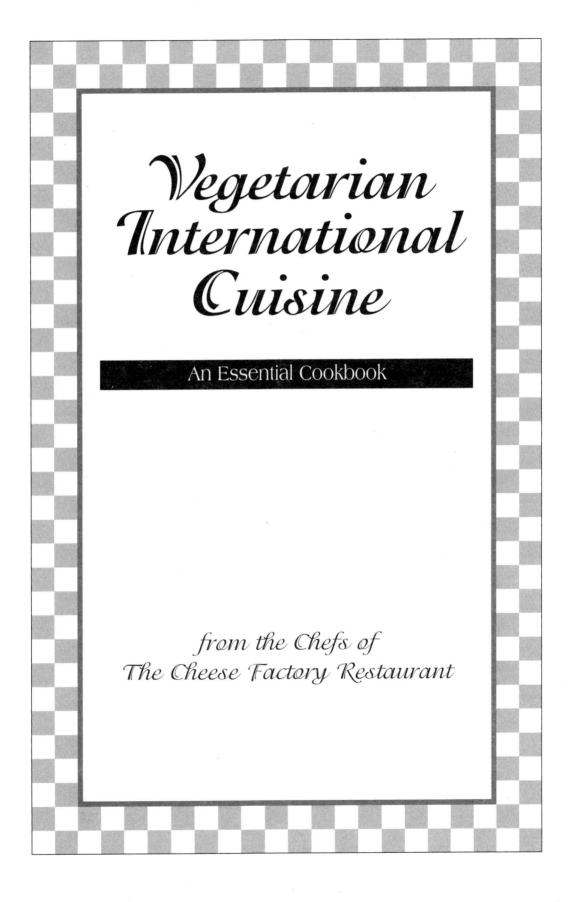

Vegetarian International Cuisine

An Essential Cookbook

from the Chefs of
The Cheese Factory Restaurant

Design and layout by
Amherst Press
A division of Palmer Publications, Inc.

Cover and interior food photographs by Bill Paulson Studios

Printed in the United States of America
by Palmer Publications, Inc.
PO Box 296
Amherst, WI 54406

Library of Congress Cataloging-in-Publication Data

Vegetarian international cuisine: an essential cookbook from the
    chefs of The Cheese Factory Restaurant
            p.   cm.
        Includes index.
        ISBN: 0-9655965-1-6
        1. Vegetarian cookery.   2. Cookery, International.
    I. Cheese Factory Restaurant.
    TX837.V4266   1997
    641.5'636—DC21   97-13995
                                                            CIP

Published in the United States of America by
The Cheese Factory Restaurant Cookbook LLC
132 Hines Terrace
Wisconsin Dells, Wisconsin 53965
(608) 253-COOK

Contents

Chapters

Introduction

America's newfound passion for ethnic flavors is one of the most dramatic food trends in its culinary evolution. In particular, the revival of vegetarian cuisines that have existed for thousands of years seems to be exploding with a contagious fervor throughout the nation.

For economic reasons as well as from long-standing tradition, the emphasis on meat is much less dominant abroad than here in the USA. Rapid transportation and volume marketing in the interstate and international commerce of foods have initiated revolutionary changes. This new age has brought us back to an appreciation for mankind's oldest foods.

At The Cheese Factory, combining different food cultures and mixing seemingly diverse ingredients comes naturally to our cooks whose backgrounds and experiences are as broad as the recipes they present. The hope is that this book will inspire and assist the reader to experience an expansion through personal culinary expressions of joie de vivre.

An in-depth exploration of cooking techniques and ingredients is beyond the scope of this book. The aim, rather, is to offer a colorful range of ideas that will ignite a creative fire deep within the heart of any cook to go far beyond the recipes in this or any book.

That being said, it is helpful to avail yourself of some basic tools of the trade. A set of good sharp knives, a blender, food processor, spice mill or small coffee grinder are essential pieces of equipment. Include an assortment of skillets, cooking pots and saucepans with covers. The best cooking pots have either a stainless steel or porcelain interior. Glass is also a good material for baking and casseroles.

A well-stocked pantry may initially seem to be an intimidating financial investment but with most high-quality products, a little goes a long way. Once you begin to appreciate the nuances of a fine virgin olive oil or a supreme aged wine vinegar, there will be no turning back.

In addition, becoming acquainted with unfamiliar or uncommon products is an adventure destined to illuminate and invigorate your food horizons. Perhaps you are simply looking for interesting, tasty, meatless recipes that are healthy, inexpensive, convenient to store and easy to prepare. This collection contains many dishes that fulfill just such a quest, along with some that reflect a desire to imitate the taste and texture of meat as well as others including no "meaty" ideas whatsoever.

The widespread interest in lighter, low-fat cooking is a trend that begs to be addressed. For more information on converting to low-fat or no-fat dishes, refer to the guidelines on page 184.

Our love affair with fresh herbs and spices and bright, bold vibrant flavors are showcased in a savory bouquet of internationally inspired dishes. An enormous treasury of assorted vegetables and fruits; pastas and noodles; potatoes and squashes; leafy lettuce greens; crunchy nuts; grains; cheeses; dairy products and eggs; grain and soybean based protein alternatives make the world of vegetarian cooking a sparkling new/old frontier where the idea of sacrificing good taste for health or wealth is merely a joke to the wise.

Above all, remember to have fun. Dance and sing through these recipes. Hop and skip with the spices; do a dip with the sauces; twirl with the pastas and harmonize with the soups. Lose or find yourself in a symphony of flavors, aromas, textures and vibrant colors. You are the maestro. Join your friends; share your masterpieces.

Chapter 1

An Introduction to Meat Substitutes

Introduction to Meat Substitutes

Tofu

A question most frequently posed by those contemplating the idea of a meatless diet is, "where's the protein?" The answer is, "it's in the beans–soybeans that is." The average protein content of most beans is 22 percent by weight, while the soybean, sometimes referred to as "the cow of the East," is 40 percent protein.

Soy protein includes all of the eight essential amino acids in a configuration readily usable by the human body. It is now widely known that there is no essential difference between plant and animal proteins. From the body's point of view, the amount of usable protein contained in one-half cup of soybeans is no different from that contained in five ounces of steak.

Soybean foods are inexpensive, extremely low in calories, contain no cholesterol and are easy to digest. These scientifically documented facts have been understood intuitively throughout East Asia since earliest times. Discovered in China more than 2000 years ago, tofu has served as the mainstay of Oriental vegetarian diets.

The production of tofu is a relatively simple process similar to that of cheese making. Soybeans are soaked, ground and boiled. This mixture is then pressed to extract the soy milk, which can be curdled or coagulated with a "salt" (such as nigari or a magnesium chloride), or an acid (such as lemon juice or vinegar). The soy milk separates into curds and whey, and the curds are then pressed into tofu.

The two most popular types of tofu in America are Japanese-style tofu and Chinese-style tofu. The Chinese tofu is considerably more compact (it is pressed longer with a heavier weight and thus contains less water). It has a more meaty texture and its consistency makes it ideally suited to an endless variation of uses. It can be marinated, baked, broiled, barbecued, braised, boiled, sauced and gravied. It can be fried, sautéed, mashed or diced. Tofu readily absorbs flavors, an endearing quality which makes it fun for the creative cook to tinker with.

In addition, a wide variety of interesting, tasty tofu products are available at most natural food markets, Oriental markets and some local supermarkets. These include grilled tofu, deep-fried tofu cutlets, savory-baked tofu, tofu frankfurters, tofu burgers, tofu pudding and more.

Keep tofu under constant refrigeration covered in plenty of water. To prolong its shelf life, drain the tofu and add fresh water daily. Regular tofu will keep seven to ten days and can be refreshed by parboiling or deep-frying. Freezing tofu radically alters its consistency, leaving it spongy and unsuitable for recipes requiring smooth and chewy textures.

Basic Preliminary Tofu Preparation

All tofu dishes served at The Cheese Factory call for water-packed, extra-firm tofu that has been drained, pressed, deep-fried and marinated before being incorporated into the various recipes. This process imparts a delicious, juicy flavor and firm, chewy meaty texture reminiscent of chicken, to the tofu. In addition, several different "cuts" of tofu are employed based on unique, aesthetic presentation of individual dishes.

Use the following instructions when preparing recipes calling for tofu:

To press tofu: Open box, drain liquid and wrap tofu in paper towels. Place a rack over a shallow pan and lay tofu on rack. Cover with heavy dinner plates and let stand 30 minutes.

To cut tofu: Remove paper towels from tofu and select appropriate cut from drawings below.

Skewer-cut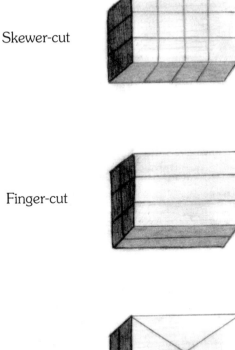

Finger-cut

Chicken-cut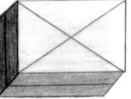

(diagrams continued on next page)

Stuffed-cut

Step A: Cut block into
        quarters.

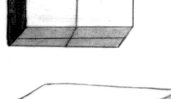

Stuffed-cut

Step B: Hollow each quarter
        to form a pocket.

Oriental-cut

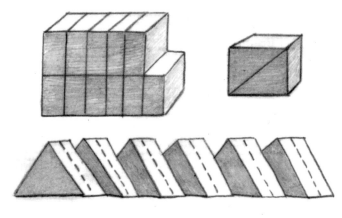

To deep-fry tofu: After tofu has been pressed and cut, deep-fry at 350 degrees F until lightly golden. Oriental-cut should be deep-fried for 1 minute; all other cuts should be deep-fried for 2 1/2 minutes. This can be done efficiently if no more than 1/3 of the cooking surface is covered at a time. If more surface area is covered, the temperature of the oil will drop resulting in an inferior product. Drain on paper towels.

To marinate tofu: Combine 3 cups boiling water with 3/4 cup vegetarian chicken-flavored powder in a bowl. Add fried tofu and marinate. All cuts except the Oriental cut should be marinated 90 minutes. The Oriental cut, being considerably smaller than the rest, is marinated 30 minutes. Marinade can be strained and frozen to reuse. Drain tofu on paper towels. Use immediately or store in sealed container in refrigerator for five days.

A Note About Vegetarian Chicken and Beef-Flavored Soup Powders

Vegetarian chicken and beef-flavored powders are used extensively at the restaurant as flavor boosters. All the recipes in this book have been tested with Flavor Gem, a commercial product available in most local supermarkets. If this brand is unavailable in your area, Washington Golden, Minors, LeGout or any other brand will do. Natural food markets generally carry a line of flavor-enhanced soup powders. Keep in mind that the salt content and flavor intensity will vary with different brands, so taste testing and seasoning adjustments are recommended.

Texturized Vegetable Protein (TVP)

Texturized vegetable or soy protein, as it is often referred to, has been developed in the West using high-level technology during the past several decades. It contains 52 percent protein and is made from defatted soy flour, extruded under great pressure and heat to form small chunks that resemble Grapenuts, although the color and shape do vary. The recipes in this book are based on the nugget type, 1/8 to 1/4 inches in diameter. When hydrated, they have a chewy, meatlike texture ideal as a ground beef substitute.

These little gems contribute a wellspring of inventive options to any cook–professional or novice, and their value cannot be overstated. Low in calories, inexpensive and non-perishable, they absorb flavors readily while retaining a firm, chewy texture. Soy products generally absorb much more flavor from herbs and spices than does meat—in many cases up to 50 percent more. Because TVP requires basically little or no cooking (only hydrating and flavoring), it can be added to any dish towards the end of the cooking time.

Contained in the Entrées chapter of this book are several thought starters or fundamental ideas on the various uses of TVP developed by our cooks. The hope is that you will be inspired to convert favorite ground beef recipes using TVP as an alternative.

Tempeh

Tempeh is Indonesia's staple soy protein food made of cultured soybeans. The beans are hulled, split and pressed into compact white cakes or patties about 3/4 inch thick. Tempeh can also be made of seeds, grains and other beans. Sold fresh, refrigerated or frozen, these cakes are usually sliced and fried until crisp and golden brown but can also be marinated, charbroiled, baked, sautéed or steamed.

The firm, meaty flavor and texture of tempeh adapts to a host of favorite Western recipes including tempeh burgers, tempeh tuna fish, tempeh chicken salad sandwiches and so on. Crispy fried cubes of tempeh are wonderful additions to salads, soups, stir-frys, casseroles, pizza or grains.

Seitan

Seitan is an ancient Oriental food staple made from wheat. High in protein and fiber but also low in fat and calories, this product is a perfect transitional food for aspiring vegetarians because it has the texture and stomach-filling heartiness of meat.

A wheat gluten product (also called wheat meat), seitan was developed by Buddhist monks about 500 years ago. Wheat gluten (the protein part of the grain) remains after washing the starch and bran out of dough made from wheat flour and water. The dough is then cut into various shapes and sizes or left whole and simmered in a savory broth for several hours.

The traditional method of making seitan is rather labor intensive and pre-cooked seitan, available at most natural food stores, is expensive to buy (running from $4 to $8 a pound). Consequently, at The Cheese Factory we use a Seitan Quick-Mix (Arrowhead Mills available at natural food stores) that if pressure cooked can be ready in 40 minutes and costs about half as much as pre-cooked seitan. In addition, it may be prepared in large batches and frozen until needed or refrigerated for one week.

Seitan was introduced into the United States through the Mormons and Seventh Day Adventists when the Japanese macrobiotic movement made its way here in the '40s. It has a long history among the Korean, Russian, Middle Eastern and other Eastern nationalities and is now becoming a staple of a balanced vegetarian diet.

Nutritionally, seitan compares favorably to both meat and tofu: a third of a pound provides almost a full day's minimum requirement of protein yet contains only 140 calories. (To get the same amount of protein from pot roast, you would have to eat twice the number of calories.)

Another astonishing fact is seitan's environmental and social benefits—the same acre of land that produces a 77-day supply of beef protein can produce 877 day's worth of wheat protein. Seitan's admirable qualities make it a superb substitute for red meats in the translation of classic recipes.

At The Cheese Factory, the use of seitan has given birth to a host of internationally-inspired dishes as well as traditional American favorites. (See Chapter 8: Entrées.)

Chapter 2

Our Kitchen Gardens

Our Kitchen Gardens

One of the unique characteristics of The Cheese Factory is the herb gardens. Set in a tranquil Wisconsin valley, not far from the restaurant, some of the most delicate fresh herbs and edible flowers used daily in the menu are lovingly tended by our staff. Customers are often surprised when the waiter explains that the lemon marigold and apricot nasturtium garnishes are not only completely edible but quite delicious.

Our growing season begins in early spring and ends in autumn. A selection of specialty produce, including Spanish pole beans and fiery Bulgarian carrots, Thai Dragon and Cascabella chilies, are cultivated to be used in many of the specials served at the restaurant. Many varieties of herbs, edible flowers and specialty produce grown in the gardens are not readily available in most grocery stores, and it gives us great pleasure to share them with our guests.

Herbs

There is no substitute for the intensely fragrant flavors contributed to a dish by the inclusion of these heavenly scented plants. Fresh herbs should be added in the last five minutes of cooking, as heat will dissipate their delicate flavors. In addition, fresh herbs can be employed to create oil and vinegar essences, which may be incorporated into dressings and sauces. The whole fresh leaves of herbs, such as Italian parsley, dill, cilantro or basil, can be tossed into mixed lettuce greens to generate unexpected excitement in dinner salads. Homemade pesto is an example of a natural and essential vehicle to showcase an abundance of fresh herbs.

All fresh herbs may be dried and stored in glass jars; or chopped, covered with olive oil and frozen for future use. Dried herbs, being concentrated, are considerably more potent than fresh and should be employed discretely. A general rule of thumb for conversion from fresh to dried herbs is four to one (i.e., if a recipe calls for four teaspoons fresh herbs, use one teaspoon dried herbs.)

Crumbling dried herbs between fingertips or crushing them in the palm of the hand releases their savory oils. Be aware when buying dried herbs—they lose flavor rapidly when exposed to light, air or heat and may be tasteless. A tired, dried herb won't do much for your recipe.

The following herbs, among many others, are prized and commonly and copiously used in our kitchen:

Basil — Virtually unknown outside of southern Europe 30 years ago, it is now rapidly on its way to becoming the most popular herb in America. The flavor is almost addictive, and there is little that a bit of basil cannot improve.

Cilantro — Sometimes called "Chinese parsley," cilantro is the leaf of the coriander plant, which is used heavily in Asian and Hispanic cuisine. Those who taste it either love it or hate it due to its unique and authentic pungent bouquet.

Dill — An ancient herb with a light, fresh, sweet scent that is incomparably delicate.

Italian parsley — Also called neapolitan parsley, this variety is far more aromatic than the widely known curly parsley found in most supermarkets. It brings out the flavor of other herbs and spices and seems to lessen the need for salt in soups, stocks and sauces.

Mint — Spearmint is the variety generally used in Middle Eastern cuisine, while peppermint, which has a warm and spicy flavor, is mostly employed in desserts and sweet dishes. Both varieties can be steeped for tea and make beautiful, fresh garnishes.

Oregano — Greek oregano is sweet and strong–an essential ingredient for Mediterranean dishes using tomato sauce as well as the type preferred for European and Slavic cooking. Mexican oregano is more pungent and perfectly suited to the spicy, hot, cumin-flavored dishes of Central and South America and the Caribbean.

Rosemary — It has been harvested from the wild for thousands of years and has a savory, minty, pine-like flavor perfect for marinades and meaty dishes.

Sage — It has one of the richest and most distinctive flavors of all herbs. Its savory strength lends admirable depth to a host of foods from soups, stews, stuffings and grains to sauces, gravies, marinades and dressings.

French Tarragon — This herb is rich, robust and slightly anise flavored. Popular in French cooking, it is often used to bring out the taste of other herbs, in herb mixes, for soups and sauces.

Thyme — Ancient Greeks considered it a symbol of style, elegance and courage. It has a vibrant flavor with a special affinity for meaty dishes. Truly one of the best all-round cooking herbs in the world.

The Art of Seasoning

The single most important factor at the heart of culinary adventure is the use of good ingredients. High-quality products ensure the cook a fair chance of achieving appetizing results.

The artistry involved in learning about flavoring food evolves with a little knowledge, experience and a lot of passionate enthusiasm. Do not be inhibited by the fear of failure—some of the best dishes at The Cheese Factory started out as mistakes.

The preferred level of seasoning is undoubtedly highly individual—especially in regard to salt. Most people enjoy flavors that are familiar to them, and the idea of broadening the range of possibilities may initially seem somewhat daunting. Some on the other hand, relish the opportunity to plunge into an exploration and appreciation of the tiniest nuances contained in a new dish. Above all, expanding the scope of the palate adds new dimensions of flavor to life. The enjoyment of each tasty moment is always available through the art of converting basic fresh elements into mouthwatering masterpieces.

Before adding herbs or spices to contribute aroma to a dish, it is important to understand several key factors. The tastes actually discerned in the mouth are sweet, sour, salt, alkaline or metallic, pungent or chili-hot, bitter or astringent.

Cold reduces sweet and sour tastes, while saltiness is increased by cold. Freezing destroys cell tissue in certain plants, an action which will also make a dish with pepper in it more peppery after freezing. The spicy taste attractive to many, cannot be

tolerated by some. Therefore freshly ground pepper, which is always optional, should be added last to taste.

Heat enhances taste by releasing aromatic oils in herbs and spices. A wide range of simple cooking techniques are employed at the restaurant to enhance and extract natural flavors and textures. Charbroiling, grilling, roasting, sautéing, braising, baking, stir-frying, smoking and marinating are among many methods represented in the following recipes. A vegetable which is quickly fried will not taste the same as one which has been stewed, steamed or grilled. A cook can take advantage of these possibilities to produce the desired result.

In the event of seasoning miscalculations, here are several suggestions to help repair the damage:

Too bitter — Add fat or something sweet (fruit juice, fruit preserves, sugar, honey, maple syrup).

Too salty — Add liquid (water, milk, juice, stock), or fat (oil, butter, cream, nut butters), or something bland (potatoes, grains, breadcrumbs) or wash off the salt.

Too sour — Add fat, salt, liquid or something sweet.

Too spicy — Add fat, something sweet, something bland or something sour.

Too sweet — Add liquid, fat or salt.

Spices

Spices are aromatic flavorings that are best enjoyed when they are slightly crushed and/or lightly toasted. Unlike fresh herbs, spices are organic substances that are often difficult to eat in their raw form. They should be treated as a food ingredient and thoroughly cooked either prior to being added to the food or added and cooked with the food.

For maximum aromatic performance, purchase spices in whole seed form and grind them in a spice mill, coffee grinder or mortar and pestle. Powdered or preground spices have already lost much of their flavor when purchased.

The particular spices most frequently used at The Cheese Factory reflect the taste preferences and general fondness for bold seasonings that our dishes are known for. They are as follows:

Allspice — The berries of a bushy evergreen shrub picked while still green and dried in the sun; this spice is native to the West Indies, Central and South America. Known in France and Spain as Jamaican pepper, it has found a place in both the savory and sweet dishes of Greece. Allspice tastes like a mixture of cloves, cinnamon and nutmeg (hence the name).

Caraway — The seeds of an herb used by ancient Greeks and Romans to season foods that were hard to digest. Today unsuspecting cooks carry on the tradition, adding caraway to breads, cabbage dishes, soups and sauces.

Cardamom — The fruit of a plant native to Southern India and used extensively in the Middle East and Europe to season baked goods and savory dishes. Cardamom is a pod consisting of an outer shell filled with tiny seeds. For milder spice flavor, the pods may be used whole—for more aromatic effect the seeds can be ground.

Cinnamon — The inner skin of fragrant young cassia tree bark—one of the oldest and most flavorful spices known to man; it grows wild throughout Asia. Depending on the intensity of flavoring required in a dish, cinnamon is used as whole sticks, crushed or ground.

Cloves — The dried buds of a tree known as Eugenia *aromatica*, which became the basis of the spice trade. Native to Southeast Asia, cloves will only thrive in a tropical climate near the ocean. Popular as a sweet baking spice, its preserving qualities make it invaluable for pickling and barbecuing.

Coriander — The seeds of the same plant, which yield fresh cilantro leaves, is the most extensively used spice in Indian cooking. This pungent-smelling white pepper-like spice is the primary ingredient in curry blends.

Cumin — The strongly aromatic seeds of an herb used widely in Latin America, North Africa, the Middle East, Asia and Spain. The unbeatable combination of roasted cumin, fresh cilantro and chipotle is found in many of The Cheese Factory's favorite recipes.

Curry — Is a blend of several spices including cumin, coriander, chili, mustard, turmeric and pepper. In India curry powders are rarely used, as it is preferred to mix the whole spices separately for each dish and grind them by hand. Curry powder was developed for the sailors of the British East India Company who had grown fond of the complexly spiced dishes while they plied their trade in the India of the late 1600s. The pre-mixed powder was an easy way to take the flavor of India home with them.

Fennel — One of the oldest of all cultivated plants, the seeds have been used for culinary and medicinal purposes since the time of the Romans. Strongly anise flavored, this spice is widely used in savory meat dishes, sauces, marinades, grains and vegetables.

Gingerroot — Is the pungent, lemony, aromatic root of a tropical plant relished as a seasoning throughout India and the Orient. In the spring a fresh crop of tender, young ginger arrives in the market from Hawaii. This "green" ginger does not need peeling and gives off a wonderful delicate aroma that is preferred in relishes, salad dressings and salsas. It is also fiberless with a texture like water chestnuts. Mature ginger must be peeled before being used for cooking.

Nutmeg — Is the oval fruit of a tropical plant found encased in a basket-like structure, which is known as mace when dry. Nutmeg goes well with spinach and cheese dishes, in cream sauces, baked goods, fresh fruit and atop hot beverages.

Sesame — The seed of a plant that has been cultivated in India since ancient times is the richest in protein, and hence is one of the primary foods in a vegetarian diet. It is used in savory and sweet dishes, ground into a paste to make tahini, and toasted and pressed to yield a highly fragrant, caramel-colored oil used throughout Asia.

Toasting Nuts and Spices

Nuts and seeds are rich in protein, vitamins and minerals. Used as both food and flavoring, they can be incorporated to thicken creamy, smooth sauces, to enrich puddings, to garnish vegetables, grains, casseroles, pastas and salads, not to mention their invaluable contribution to desserts and baked goods.

Nuts and seeds contain a large portion of oil and must be stored in a cool, dry place to prevent them from turning rancid. For best flavor, purchase nuts from stores with a quick turnover, and do not store them for longer than six months. Toasting nuts and seeds brings out their delicate characteristics and makes them even more delicious. We recommend the following basic instructions:

To toast nuts and seeds: (including almonds, cashews, hazelnuts, macadamias, pecans, pine nuts, pumpkin seeds, sesame seeds, sunflower seeds, walnuts), preheat oven to 350 degrees F. Place nuts or seeds in a shallow baking pan or on a cookie sheet and toast until they smell nutty and are slightly golden in color (5 to 10 minutes). Remove from heat; cool, chop, grind or leave whole according to recipe directions. Store in sealed container.

To toast spices: (primarily cumin seeds and coriander seeds), toast spices in a dry skillet over medium-high heat until slightly darkened and fragrant (1 to 2 minutes). Remove from heat; cool and grind or leave whole according to recipe directions. Store in sealed container.

Peppers

Peppers are adored by countless cultures and cuisines throughout the world to add taste, texture, color and heat to food. There are an enormous variety of peppers whose names change from one place to another—(the Mexican name for pepper is chili). Many markets now stock a variety including large green poblanos, medium-size jalapeños and tiny serranos. The rule of thumb is the larger the pepper, the sweeter and milder the taste; the smaller the pepper, the hotter the taste.

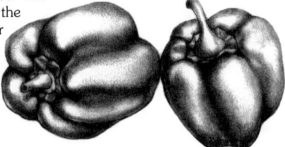

Whether using peppers fresh, dried or canned, keep in mind that all the flavor is in the pulp—the seeds are indigestible and carry no taste.

Oils

One factor that gives various dishes and cuisines their individual character is the use of distinctly different cooking oils. The taste of a simple dish, such as quick sautéed spinach, can be radically altered based on the type of oil used. Cold, pressed unrefined oils are the most intensely aromatic.

Dark sesame oil — Made from toasted sesame seeds, this strong, full-flavored oil is more of a seasoning element than a cooking oil since it is so intensely flavored and burns at a very low temperature. It's prone to rancidity, so buy a small bottle and keep it refrigerated.

Olive oil — Extra-virgin refers to the first pressing of oil extracted from olives by mechanical means without the use of heat or chemicals. Dark and flavorful, virgin olive oil is a seasoning element in its own right. Light or pure olive oil is a grade produced from successive pressings. Store olive oil tightly sealed away from the light.

Peanut oil — Peanut oil is recommended for frying since it doesn't smoke or burn until it reaches a high temperature.

Vegetable oil — Canola, peanut or safflower are good in recipes that call for light vegetable oil.

Walnut or hazelnut oils — These nut oils elevate crisp salads to dazzling new heights. They are expensive, but a little goes a long way. Fragile nut oils turn rancid faster than other oils and should be kept refrigerated.

Vinegars

Assorted fruit and herb vinegars — These are good flavor enhancers in many vinaigrettes providing they are of good quality.

Balsamic vinegar — Balsamic vinegar is produced in Modena, Italy, and is made from the juice of Trebbiano grapes. Traditionally aged, sometimes for decades in a succession of barrels of different woods, this tart, sweet, rich ingredient is unique and versatile—essential in any kitchen.

Citrus juices and zest — May be used in place of vinegar or combined with vinegar to brighten vinaigrettes and dressings.

Red wine vinegar — A high-quality, aged red wine vinegar bears no resemblance to the poor-quality version found in most supermarkets. A trip to a specialty store for this essential ingredient is recommended.

Rice wine vinegar — Light, clean tasting and slightly sweet, this vinegar is perfect in a variety of Asian dishes.

Sherry vinegar — A fine Spanish sherry vinegar produces aromatic, mouthwatering vinaigrettes and marinades.

Chapter 3

Appetizers

Roasted Red and Yellow Peppers

These vibrant, flaming peppers may be sampled in a myriad of ways. Great as a garnish on vegetable, grain or pasta dishes, they are luxurious in sandwiches, on pizza or in quiche. Their savory goodness is an essential addition to an antipasto tray. Peppers may also be puréed in a blender and used as a sauce. They will keep well in the refrigerator for five days.

Yield: 6 marinated roasted peppers

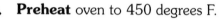

3 medium red peppers
   (approximately 1 1/2 pounds)
3 medium yellow peppers
   (approximately 1 1/2 pounds)
2 tablespoons olive oil

Marinade:
1/2 cup olive oil
2 teaspoons dried oregano,
   crumbled
2 teaspoons whole fennel seeds
1 teaspoon salt
1 teaspoon freshly ground
   black pepper
2 teaspoons minced garlic

Preheat oven to 450 degrees F.

Rub peppers with oil; place on oven rack over shallow baking pan. Roast 15 to 20 minutes; turn peppers and continue roasting an additional 20 minutes or until skins begin to char and crack and peppers collapse. (The flesh should remain tender but firm, not mushy.) To maintain bright color, do not allow to darken too much. Place hot peppers into a container; seal and steam 1 hour. (This will facilitate removal of the skins and seeds.)

To make marinade, combine oil, oregano, fennel seeds, 1 teaspoon salt or to taste, pepper and garlic in a small bowl. Mix well; set aside.

Remove skins and seeds from peppers; discard. Tear peppers into 2-inch strips; place in marinade 2 to 4 hours before serving.

Marinated Eggplant Stuffed with Chèvre

This is a lovely dish reminiscent of a Mediterranean breeze. Feta may be substituted for the chèvre, and seasoned leftover rice or mushrooms render a fine filling alternative. Toss in a little Italian Crumble Sausage (page 133) and serve warm with Marinara Sauce (page 58). Bon appétit!

Yield: 18 to 20 rolls

2 medium eggplant
  (1 pound each)
2 teaspoons salt
1/4 cup olive oil
1 pound chèvre cheese

Marinade:
2 large cloves garlic,
  peeled and minced
1/4 cup fresh Italian parsley, packed
1/4 cup fresh basil leaves, packed
1 cup good-quality olive oil
1/3 cup balsamic or good-quality
  red wine vinegar
Salt and pepper

Preheat oven to 375 degrees F.

Cut eggplant lengthwise into 1/4-inch-thick slices. Salt slices lightly on both sides. Place on rack over shallow pan; drain 1 hour.

Rinse eggplant slices and pat dry. Oil a heavy cookie sheet; arrange eggplant in single layer. Brush eggplant on both sides with oil and bake 5 minutes on each side. Remove from oven and cool.

Spread each slice with chèvre and roll into tube shapes. Place tubes in a shallow glass dish.

To make marinade, combine garlic, parsley, basil, oil and vinegar in blender; process until herbs are minced. Season marinade with salt and pepper, as desired; pour over eggplant rolls. Chill overnight. Serve at room temperature.

Middle Eastern Stuffed Tomatoes

This appetizer is eye-catching on a buffet, pretty when served as an appetizer or can be used as a garnish on an entrée, such as Moroccan Shish Kabobs (page 142). Use the filling as a dip for crisp vegetables or spread on toasted pita bread. Try a combination platter of Sfeeha (Syrian Meat Pies) (page 20), Baked Stuffed Mushrooms (page 21) and Middle Eastern Stuffed Tomatoes.

Yield: 8 stuffed tomatoes

Tomatoes:
- 8 large roma tomatoes
- 2 teaspoons salt

Eggplant:
- 1 large eggplant
- 1 tablespoon olive oil

Stuffing:
- 1 tablespoon minced garlic
- 1 1/2 tablespoons finely chopped scallions
- 1 tablespoon chopped fresh mint, packed or chopped fresh Italian parsley, packed
- 1 1/2 tablespoons mayonnaise
- 1 tablespoon olive oil
- 1 tablespoon dried rosemary leaves, ground in spice grinder, coffee mill or mortar and pestle
- 1/2 teaspoon salt
- 1/2 teaspoon freshly ground black pepper
- Zest of 1/2 lemon
- 2 tablespoons fresh lemon juice

To prepare tomatoes, lay tomato on its side and slice off top third, reserving top for lid. Cut off a thin strip from opposite side (this will be the bottom), so that tomato will stand flat after it has been stuffed. Repeat process with remaining tomatoes. Using a melon baller, hollow out tomatoes and lightly salt cavities. Invert tomatoes on a small rack in a shallow baking pan. Allow to drain 1 hour.

Preheat oven to 400 degrees F.

To prepare eggplant, cut stem and bottom off eggplant and discard. Peel and cut lengthwise in 1/2-inch-thick slices. Brush both sides with oil and place on a cookie sheet. Bake about 20 minutes or until eggplant is tender. Remove from heat and cool.

To prepare stuffing, chop tomato pulp and place in a small bowl. Add garlic, scallions, mint, mayonnaise, oil, rosemary, salt, pepper, lemon zest and juice. Mix well. Chill at least 2 hours before using.

Fill tomatoes with stuffing, placing reserved tomato lids on top at a slight angle to expose filling.

Lettuce Bundles

This version of one of America's most popular luncheon items may be enjoyed as a chicken salad on a bed of greens, in a sandwich or as one of several items on a combination platter. It makes a terrific cold hors d'oeuvre as presented in this recipe. If using iceberg lettuce, make sure leaves are large, and cut out the hard core at the base of each leaf. Swiss chard, collard or mustard greens make a perfect casing for these chicken parcels. Try using Tempeh Tuna Salad (page 78) as a filling alternative.

Yield: 16 lettuce bundles

1 package (16 ounces) extra-firm tofu
1/2 cup mayonnaise
1 package (4 ounces) cream cheese, softened
1/2 cup chopped celery
1/2 cup chopped carrots
1/2 cup chopped scallions
1 can (2 1/4 ounces) sliced black olives (1/2 cup)
1 teaspoon salt
1/2 teaspoon freshly ground black pepper
1/2 teaspoon dried marjoram, crumbled
1/2 teaspoon dried thyme, crumbled
2 large heads iceberg lettuce (16 large leaves), or 2 bunches Swiss chard, collard or mustard greens (16 large leaves)

Press moisture from tofu; slice in chicken-cut fashion, deep-fry and marinate according to instructions (page 3). Cut prepared tofu into 1/2-inch pieces and place in a large bowl. In a small bowl, combine mayonnaise and cream cheese; add to tofu. Add celery, carrots, scallions, olives, 1 teaspoon salt or to taste, pepper, marjoram and thyme. Mix well to combine.

Place 1/3 cup of mixture in bottom center of each leaf and roll up half way. (If using Swiss chard, collard or mustard greens, lightly steam leaves first and chill before rolling.) Fold in sides and finish rolling. Place on serving platter seam side down. Refrigerate until ready to use.

Sfeeha

(Syrian Meat Pies)

Here's an excellent use for texturized vegetable protein (TVP) to create a delicious savory-filled pastry. Substitute any favorite pie crust recipe including phyllo (follow directions on package for handling and wrapping). Serve with Cucumber Yogurt Sauce (page 51).

Yield: 16 meat pies

4 tablespoons raisins
1/2 recipe Meat Mother (approximately 2 1/2 cups) (page 127)
1/2 cup slivered toasted almonds or pine nuts (page 12)
1 cup finely chopped onion
Juice of 1 lemon
1/2 teaspoon salt
1/2 teaspoon ground black pepper
1/2 teaspoon allspice
1/2 teaspoon curry powder
1 teaspoon roasted ground cumin (page 13)
1/4 teaspoon cinnamon
2 tablespoons pitted and sliced kalamata olives
2 packages (8 ounces each) crescent roll dough*
2 large eggs
2 tablespoons cold water
4 tablespoons sesame seeds

Soften raisins in 1/2 cup warm water for 5 minutes. Drain and discard water; set aside.

Preheat oven to 350 degrees F.

Combine Meat Mother with raisins, nuts, onion, lemon juice, salt, pepper, allspice, curry powder, cumin, cinnamon and olives in a large bowl; mix well. Place 2 tablespoons filling on each piece of dough; bring corners together up over filling. Pinch dough together with fingers and twist to create a nice finish. Beat eggs with water in a small bowl. Brush each pie with egg wash and sprinkle with sesame seeds. Place on a cookie sheet and bake 10 to 15 minutes or until golden brown and cooked through.

*Available in refrigerated section of local supermarkets.

Baked Stuffed Mushrooms

Perfect as an appetizer or side dish, these mushrooms are hearty enough to be offered as a main course on a bed of buttered linguine or with a crisp salad and some of your favorite garlic bread. The stuffing may be featured as a filling for other vegetables, such as eggplant, zucchini or tomatoes.

Yield: 24 baked stuffed mushrooms

24 large white button mushrooms
      (2 to 3 inches in diameter)
1/4 cup butter
  2 tablespoons olive oil
1/4 cup minced onion
  2 tablespoons minced garlic
1/2 cup white wine
  2 tablespoons Worcestershire sauce
  2 tablespoons vegetarian beef-
      flavored powder
  2 tablespoons boiling water
  2 cups cooked wild rice
1 1/2 cups coarsely chopped walnuts
  2 tablespoons fresh Italian parsley,
      finely chopped, packed
  1 teaspoon salt
  1 teaspoon freshly ground
      black pepper
  2 teaspoons ground nutmeg
  1 teaspoon paprika
1/4 cup butter, melted
1/2 cup good-quality grated
      Parmesan cheese

Remove mushroom stems and mince; set aside 1 cup. Wipe mushroom caps with a damp cloth and set aside.

Heat butter and oil in a 10-inch skillet; add onion and garlic. Sauté until translucent. Add minced stems and sauté until most of the liquid has evaporated. Add wine and Worcestershire; cook 2 minutes more. Dissolve vegetarian beef-flavored powder in boiling water and add to skillet. Stir in rice, walnuts, parsley, 1 teaspoon salt or to taste, 1 teaspoon pepper or to taste, nutmeg and paprika; simmer 3 to 4 minutes. Remove from heat and cool.

Brush mushroom caps with butter; turn over and fill with stuffing. Place on a cookie sheet or baking pan, filling side up. Broil 3 minutes. Remove from oven and sprinkle tops with cheese. Return to broiler for an additional 2 to 3 minutes.

Garnish with a little marinated Roasted Red and Yellow Peppers (page 16).

Variation: Omit vegetarian beef-flavored powder and water; replace with 2 tablespoons soy sauce mixed with 2 tablespoons water.

Lemon Tarragon Mushrooms

These magical mushrooms are bursting with flavor excitement like little explosions of delight in each mouthful! The stuffing mixture can be prepared one to two days ahead and refrigerated until ready to use. The remaining marinade may be enjoyed as a vinaigrette on salads or vegetables. It will keep in the refrigerator for several weeks.

Yield: 24 stuffed mushrooms

Marinade:
- 4 lemons, zest and juice
- 1/4 cup minced garlic
- 2 cups olive oil
- 4 cups rice vinegar*
- 1 tablespoon salt
- 1/4 cup Worcestershire sauce
- 1 cup coarsely chopped fresh tarragon, packed, or 1 tablespoon dried tarragon, crumbled

Stuffing:
- 24 large white button mushrooms with stems (2 inches in diameter)
- 10 ounces additional mushrooms
- 2 ounces dried shiitake mushrooms,* stems removed and discarded
- 2 cups hot water
- 4 tablespoons olive oil
- 2 cups chopped onion
- 2 tablespoons minced garlic
- 1/4 cup brandy
- 2 tablespoons Worcestershire sauce
- 1/2 cup chopped fresh tarragon, tightly packed, or 2 teaspoons dried tarragon, crumbled
- 2 cups cooked white rice
- 1 lemon, zest and juice
- 1 cup slivered toasted almonds (page 12)
- 2 teaspoons salt
- 1/2 teaspoon ground nutmeg
- 1/2 teaspoon coarsely ground black pepper

*Available in Oriental markets.

To make marinade, in a large bowl, combine lemon zest and juice, garlic, oil, vinegar, salt, Worcestershire and tarragon; stir.

Remove stems from large mushrooms and reserve. Using a melon baller, scoop out a little of the mushroom flesh from cavity. Wipe mushroom caps with damp paper towel and immerse in marinade 2 to 3 hours. Combine and finely chop mushroom flesh with stems and additional 10 ounces mushrooms. There should be a total of 5 cups finely chopped mushrooms.

Soak shiitake mushrooms in hot water until softened, about 20 minutes. Drain, discard water and finely chop.

Heat oil in a 10-inch skillet; sauté onions and garlic for 2 to 3 minutes. (If using dried tarragon, add to onions and garlic.) Add the 5 cups finely chopped mushrooms and cook an additional 5 minutes or until liquid has evaporated. Add brandy, shiitakes and Worcestershire; cook 2 to 3 minutes. (If using fresh tarragon, add now.) Remove from heat and add rice, lemon zest and juice, almonds, salt, nutmeg and pepper. Mix and allow to cool.

To assemble, remove large mushroom caps from marinade; drain. Stuff each mushroom cap and garnish with fresh tarragon leaf and small strip of Roasted Red Pepper (page 16).

Marinated Mushrooms

An appealing array of flavors sensational on a bed of chilled rice noodles, fresh spinach or any crisp greens mix. Add to a bowl of assorted steamed and chilled vegetables including broccoli, cauliflower, carrots or baby corn for a colorful marinated collection.

Yield: 8 cups mushrooms

12 dry or fresh shiitake mushrooms,*
　　stems removed and discarded
1 1/4 pounds white button mushrooms,
　　uniform in size (about 40 to 45)

Marinade:
　2/3 cup Tamarind Ginger Garlic
　　　Sauce (page 160) or
　　　commercial hoisin sauce*
　2/3 cup vegetable oil
　6 tablespoons rice vinegar*
　1 1/2 teaspoons minced garlic
　1 tablespoon onion salt
　　Zest of 1 lemon
　　Juice of 2 lemons

If using dried shiitakes, reconstitute by placing shiitakes in a small bowl; add 2 cups boiling water. Cover and let stand 20 minutes; drain and discard water. Place in clean towel and squeeze out excess moisture.

Wipe button mushrooms with a damp paper towel and place in bowl with shiitakes.

To make marinade, in a small bowl, combine Tamarind Sauce, oil, vinegar, garlic, onion salt, lemon zest and juice; whisk. Pour over mushrooms and marinate 12 to 24 hours before serving.

*Available in local supermarkets or Oriental markets.

Egg Rolls
with Apricot-Ginger Sauce

A delicious rendition of a traditional Oriental favorite involves some preparation time but can be expedited in stages. The Tamarind Ginger Garlic Sauce (page 160) can be made several days ahead and refrigerated. The vegetable mixture may be prepared a day in advance. Large batches of egg rolls can be frozen for future use. We recommend serving hot Chinese mustard with the Apricot-Ginger Sauce.

Yield: 2 dozen egg rolls

25 dried shiitake mushrooms,*
  (1½ ounces), stems removed
  and discarded
 6 cups thinly sliced cabbage
  (do not shred or there will be
  too much moisture)
1½ cups chopped celery
1½ cups chopped carrots
1½ cups chopped scallions
 1 tablespoon minced garlic
½ tablespoon salt
¼ teaspoon ground white pepper
½ cup Tamarind Ginger Garlic
  Sauce (page 160) or
  commercial hoisin sauce*
 2 tablespoons minced fresh
  gingerroot
½ tablespoon dark sesame oil
 3 tablespoons cornstarch
 3 tablespoons cold water
24 egg roll wrappers
 2 egg whites

Place shiitakes in a bowl of boiling water; cover and set aside 20 minutes. Drain and discard water. Squeeze mushrooms in a clean towel to remove excess water. Mince shiitakes and place in a large bowl with cabbage, celery, carrots, scallions, garlic, salt, pepper, Tamarind Sauce, gingerroot and oil. Dissolve cornstarch in cold water and add to rest of ingredients. Mix well; cover and chill.

When ready to assemble follow directions on package of egg roll wrappers using ¼ cup filling per roll or place wrapper on work surface with points forming a diamond. Place ¼ cup filling on bottom point of wrapper. Roll from bottom up, stopping in middle. Fold sides in like an envelope; continue rolling to the end.

Lightly beat egg whites in a small bowl and brush rolls to seal seams. (Do not allow egg rolls to touch, or they will stick together.) After 3 to 4 rolls have been assembled, immediately deep-fry at 350 degrees F for 1½ to 2 minutes, so egg rolls are crisp, not soggy. Remove egg rolls and place in warm oven, repeating process until all rolls have been assembled and cooked.

*Available in Oriental markets.

To freeze uncooked egg rolls, line a cookie sheet or shallow pan with waxed paper. Assemble 4 to 5 egg rolls at a time and place on pan making sure rolls are not touching. Freeze immediately. Repeat assembly and freezing process until all wrappers are used.

When all rolls are completely frozen, transfer to a storage container using waxed paper between layers.

To cook, remove rolls from freezer and deep-fry 5 minutes at 350 degrees F.

Apricot-Ginger Sauce

This sauce was designed to be served with egg rolls but may also be adapted to accompany baked squash, sweet potatoes or sautéed bananas. Try it on waffles, pancakes, crêpes or cheese blintzes with fresh whipped cream or sour cream. It keeps well in the refrigerator for several weeks and freezes perfectly.

Yield: 1 pint sauce

3/4 cup apricot preserves
1/4 cup sugar
    Juice of 1 lime
1/2 cup rice vinegar*
  2 teaspoons salt
  1 tablespoon minced fresh
    gingerroot
1/4 teaspoon red pepper flakes
    (optional)

Purée preserves, sugar, lime juice, vinegar, salt, gingerroot and pepper flakes in blender until smooth. Chill.

*Available in Oriental markets.

Spring Rolls
with Thai Peanut Dipping Sauce

Serve these rolls at room temperature with Thai Peanut Dipping Sauce.
The sauce may be prepared and refrigerated several days ahead.
The lettuce can be shredded several hours in advance as long as the
cucumbers are stored separately and mixed with other ingredients just
before assembling. Practice making these before your guests arrive.
They are really very easy once you get the hang of it.
For those watching calories, this recipe is for you.

Yield: 12 to 14 rolls

2 quarts water
1 teaspoon salt
8 ounces thin white rice noodles*
1 tablespoon vegetable oil
2 cups shredded iceberg lettuce
1 quart hot water
16 rice wrappers* (8-inch rounds)
1/2 cucumber, peeled, seeded and
    diced (1 cup)
3 scallions, thinly sliced (1/2 cup)
1/4 cup fresh cilantro leaves,
    washed and patted dry

Bring 2 quarts water to a boil in a 5-quart saucepan. Add salt and cook noodles according to package directions. Drain and transfer to a small bowl; toss with oil. Chill before assembling.

Pat lettuce dry with paper towel. (Spring rolls should be assembled just before serving because wrappers tend to get rubbery.)

Pour 1 quart hot water into a bowl; dip one wrapper at a time for 3 to 5 seconds or until it softens. (It will tear if it has been in water too long.) Place wrapper on work surface. On the bottom third of wrapper, layer equal amounts of chilled rice noodles, lettuce, cucumber, scallion and cilantro leaves. Fold bottom of wrapper up and start to roll. Tuck in sides and continue rolling all the way up. Place seam side down on serving dish and cover with damp paper towel until ready to serve.

*Available in Oriental markets.

Thai Peanut Dipping Sauce

*Although created to complement spring rolls, this recipe makes
a light, low-calorie sauce for steamed vegetables and tofu.
Toss with cooked rice noodles or use as a salad dressing.
It keeps well in the refrigerator for one week.*

Yield: 1 pint sauce

1 tablespoon vegetarian chicken-
flavored powder
1/2 cup boiling water
1 cup rice vinegar*
1/3 cup sugar
1 lime leaf*
2 dried Chinese chili peppers*
1 teaspoon galanga powder*
1 tablespoon peanut oil
2 tablespoons crushed peanuts

In a small bowl, dissolve vegetarian chicken-flavored powder in boiling water. Add vinegar, sugar, lime leaf, peppers, galanga powder, oil and peanuts. Refrigerate until ready to serve.

*Available in Oriental markets.

Norimaki with Vegetables

In traditional Japanese sushi-making, the nori is prepared with a particular type of sticky rice and various kinds of raw fish. It is offered here with an assortment of vegetables and eggs. Seasoned tofu or avocado make good filling additions. The nori is best if served immediately, but it will hold well for several hours. It makes a lovely presentation on a buffet or as individual servings.
(See photo on page 97)

Yield: 4 rolls (24 pieces)

Rice:
    1 cup Calrose rice*
    1 tablespoon sugar
    1 tablespoon rice vinegar*
    1/2 teaspoon salt
    3 cups water

Eggs:
    1 teaspoon vegetable oil
    2 eggs

Vegetables:
    1 carrot (7 to 8 inches long)
    1/4 cup tamari or soy sauce
    1 cucumber (7 to 8 inches long)
    4 small scallions (7 to 8 inches long)
    4 sheets fine-quality pre-toasted
        sushi nori*
    1/2 cup toasted sesame seeds
        (page 12)

Dipping sauce:
    1/2 cup tamari or soy sauce
    1/2 cup mirin* (Japanese rice wine)
    1 inch piece finely minced fresh
        gingerroot

Wasabi: (Japanese green horseradish)
    3 tablespoons Wasabi powder*
    2 teaspoons cold water

    1 jar (12 ounces) pickled ginger*

*Available in Oriental markets.

Place rice, sugar, vinegar, salt and water in a small saucepan. Cover and slowly bring to a boil over medium heat. Reduce heat; simmer 15 to 20 minutes or until water is absorbed; remove from heat. (Rice should be quite sticky.) Transfer to a shallow glass dish; cool 20 minutes. Cover with plastic wrap and refrigerate until ready to assemble.

Heat oil in a 7-inch omelette pan; beat eggs in a small bowl and pour into prepared pan. Cook eggs omelette-style (circular shape), but do not fold in half. When eggs are firm remove from pan; allow to cool. Slice into 1/4-inch-wide strips, reserving longest strips for nori; set aside.

Peel carrot and cut into long 1/4-inch-wide strips. In a small saucepan, bring 2 cups water to a boil; add tamari. Blanch carrot strips 5 minutes or until just tender. Remove strips from pan; cool and chill in refrigerator. Peel cucumber and slice in half lengthwise. Remove seeds with melon baller or teaspoon; cut into long 1/4-inch-thick strips; set aside. Wash and trim scallions; set aside.

To assemble, have a small bowl of warm water and a bamboo sushi mat* handy. Place a sheet of nori, shiny side down, on mat. Spoon 1/4 of the chilled rice mixture (about 2/3 cup) on nori sheet; spread and press mixture out evenly, leaving a 1/4-inch border on 3 sides and a 2-inch border on top. Sprinkle 1 to 2 teaspoons sesame seeds horizontally across rice about 1/3 of the way up. Put a strip of egg over sesame seeds. Lay 1 carrot and 1 cucumber strip over egg and top with a scallion. Grasp edges of mat and nori (see diagram) together and roll, tucking firmly into center (see diagram). Continue to roll while squeezing middle to avoid a bulge and make roll even. Hold roll tightly in mat for a moment to help seal edges. (Moisture in rice will enable nori seams to stick together.)

Repeat process until all rolls have been assembled.

Serve with dipping sauce, Wasabi and pickled ginger. To make dipping sauce, combine tamari, rice wine and ginger-root in a small bowl. Sprinkle with 1 teaspoon sesame seeds. To make Wasabi, combine Wasabi powder and water in a small bowl; stir until mixture makes a thick paste. Let stand 10 minutes.

Using a wet, sharp French knife, trim ends of each roll. Cut into 6 slices; use 3 pieces as an appetizer or 6 pieces as a light entrée.

1

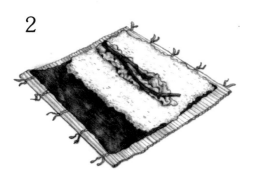

2

3

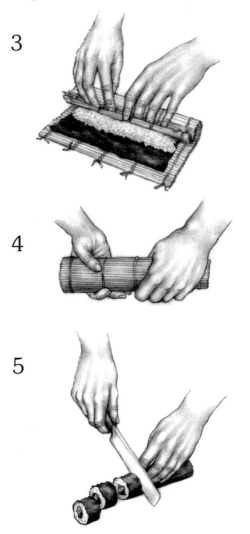

4

5

Tea Leaf Eggs

*This recipe is visually beautiful as well as delicious and easy to prepare.
Use it to adorn a brunch buffet or offer it as a light luncheon item.
Serve with Chilled Asparagus with Sesame Vinaigrette (page 72)
or Chilled Sesame Spinach (page 76).*

Yield: 8 hard-boiled eggs

1 cup Tea Leaf Egg Sauce

8 large eggs
1 1/2 tablespoons salt
5 tea bags
1/2 cup soy sauce
4 star anise*
   Water (to cover eggs by
      at least 1 inch)
1/2 cup thinly sliced scallions

Tea Leaf Egg Sauce:
   1 cup mayonnaise
   2 tablespoons tea leaf juice
   2 teaspoons Dijon mustard
   Zest of 1 lemon

Place eggs, salt, tea bags, soy sauce, star anise and water in a medium saucepan. Bring to a boil; reduce heat and simmer 3 minutes. Remove eggs from tea mixture, reserve juice; set aside. Plunge eggs into cold water to stop cooking. When cool enough to handle, tap egg shell lightly with the back of a spoon until fine cracks cover the entire surface. Place cracked eggs in pan with reserved juice; simmer gently for 2 hours. Remove pan from heat; let eggs and juice stand in pan at room temperature at least 8 hours. Reserve 2 tablespoons juice; refrigerate pan with remaining juice and eggs until ready to assemble.

To make Tea Leaf Egg Sauce, combine mayonnaise, reserved 2 tablespoons tea leaf juice, mustard and lemon zest; mix well.

To serve, shell each egg and cut in half lengthwise. Make a pool of Tea Leaf Egg Sauce (about 2 tablespoons) on a small appetizer dish; sprinkle with 1 to 2 teaspoons scallions. Place halved egg cut side down on top of sauce.

*Available in Oriental markets.

Smoked Eggs with Citrus Herb Sauce

This is a "must try" dish for the adventuresome palate. It is simply and uniquely delicious. Easy to prepare in advance; it's a show-stopper!

Yield: 8 eggs

Marinade:
- 1 cup soy sauce
- 1/4 cup liquid smoke
- 1/4 cup sugar
- 1 tablespoon salt

- 8 large hard-boiled eggs, peeled
- 1/2 cup thinly sliced scallions

To make marinade, in a small bowl, combine soy sauce, liquid smoke, sugar and salt. Place eggs in marinade for 2 hours, swishing eggs around every 30 minutes. Remove eggs and refrigerate. Freeze marinade for later use.

On a small appetizer dish make a pool of Citrus Herb Sauce (about 2 table-spoons) and sprinkle with 1 to 2 teaspoons scallions. Cut egg in half lengthwise and place cut side down on top of sauce. Garnish with sprig of fresh parsley or mint.

Citrus Herb Sauce

Yield: 1 1/2 cups sauce

- 1/2 cup mayonnaise
- 1/2 cup sour cream
- 1 tablespoon Dijon mustard
- 1 tablespoon Worcestershire sauce
  - Zest of 1 lemon (2 teaspoons)
  - Juice of 1/2 lemon (2 tablespoons)
- 2 tablespoons chopped fresh dill, packed, or 2 teaspoons dried dill, crumbled
- 2 tablespoons chopped fresh Italian parsley (do not use dried parsley)

In a small bowl, combine mayonnaise, sour cream, mustard, Worcestershire, lemon zest and juice, dill and parsley. Whisk until well blended.

Tortilla Española

This rendition of the traditional Spanish tapa is a thick omelette made from potatoes, eggs and onions. Spaniards consume huge quantities of tortillas for breakfast, lunch or dinner. In a way, it is Spain's version of the American hamburger. Its versatility enables it to be appreciated as an appetizer, side dish or entrée. The tortillas may be prepared up to two or three days in advance and kept refrigerated. To heat, place in a microwave or moderate oven until just slightly warmed through. Serve warm or at room temperature accompanied by Romesco Sauce (page 56).

Yield: 2 tortillas

1   large yellow onion (1 pound)
3 1/2   pounds Idaho potatoes
        (5 potatoes)
1/2   cup olive oil
3   teaspoons salt
12   large eggs

Preheat oven to 400 degrees F.

Peel and thinly slice onion; set aside. Peel potatoes and immerse in a bowl of cold water to retain color. Cut potatoes in half lengthwise; place cut side down and thinly slice into half-moons (1/8 inch or less); return potatoes to cold water until all are sliced. Drain potatoes; place in medium roasting pan. Add onion, 1/4 cup of the oil and 1 1/2 teaspoons of the salt. Toss with hands until potatoes and onions are well coated. Cover pan with foil; bake approximately 45 minutes or until potatoes are tender, but firm. Remove foil and allow potato mixture to cool to room temperature. (Mixture may be refrigerated at this point and completed the next day.)

In a medium bowl, beat eggs with a wire whisk. Add potato mixture and remaining 1 1/2 teaspoons salt; mix until well blended.

Preheat oven to 350 degrees F.

Heat 1 tablespoon oil in a nonstick 7- to 8-inch omelette pan until oil smokes. Add half the potato mixture; reduce heat to low. Allow mixture to set 1 minute; then place pan in oven for approximately 20 minutes. Remove from oven; invert tortilla onto a flat plate. Add 1 tablespoon oil to pan; slide tortilla back into pan, return to oven to brown other side, approximately 20 minutes. Remove from oven; invert cooked tortilla onto a flat plate. Repeat procedure with remaining potato mixture. Cool to room temperature or serve warm.

Santa Fe Bean Dip

This boldly seasoned bean dip makes an outstanding filling for burritos, enchiladas or tacos. Serve with blue and yellow corn tortilla chips, Tulsa Salsa (page 39) and Guacamole Grande (page 36). For a spicier version, try adding a little No Known Survivors (page 56). Keeps well in the refrigerator for one week and freezes perfectly.

Yield: 2$1/2$ cups

1 can (7 ounces) chipotle peppers in adobo sauce*
1 can (16 ounces) vegetarian refried beans
1/4 cup finely chopped onion
1 teaspoon minced garlic
1 tablespoon canned chopped jalapeños, drained
1/4 cup chopped fresh cilantro, packed
2 tablespoons olive oil
2 teaspoons lemon juice
1 tablespoon chili powder
1/2 teaspoon dried oregano, crumbled
1/2 teaspoon dried basil, crumbled
1/2 teaspoon roasted ground cumin (page 13)
1/8 teaspoon cayenne pepper
2 tablespoons butter
2 tablespoons heavy cream
3/4 cup shredded Cheddar cheese

Purée chipotle peppers in sauce in blender. Reserve 1 tablespoon for bean dip. (Refrigerate or freeze remaining purée for future use. Keeps for several weeks in refrigerator.)

In a medium bowl, mix together reserved 1 tablespoon puréed chipotle, beans, onion, garlic, jalapeños, cilantro, oil, lemon juice, chili powder, oregano, basil, cumin and cayenne.

Melt butter in a small saucepan over low heat; add cream and cheese, stirring until cheese melts. Remove from heat and stir into bean mixture; combine well. Chill until ready to serve.

Note: For best results, we use the San Marcos brand of chipotle peppers in adobo sauce.

*Available in Hispanic markets.

Hummus

Drizzle a little virgin olive oil on top of this Middle Eastern dip and serve with toasted pita bread, kalamata olives, sliced tomatoes, cucumbers and onions. Garnish with fresh parsley or mint. Make it part of a combination platter with tabbouleh and baba ghanouj. Enjoy it as a filling for tomatoes or a dip for crudités. It keeps well in the refrigerator four to five days and can be prepared in large quantities, portioned into storage containers and frozen.

Yield: 3 1/2 cups

1 1/2 pounds canned garbanzo beans (1 1/2 quarts), drained; reserve 1/2 cup plus 2 tablespoons liquid
2 teaspoons minced garlic
3 tablespoons lemon juice
3/4 cup roasted tahini*
1/4 cup vegetable oil
1 teaspoon salt

In a large bowl, combine beans, reserved juice, garlic, lemon juice, tahini, oil and 1 teaspoon salt or to taste. Purée in batches in food processor until very smooth.

Cover and chill or freeze until ready to serve.

*Available in natural food markets.

Spinach Dip

Serve this dip in a hollowed out loaf of rye bread or head of red cabbage. It also can be enjoyed as a spread on a sandwich. Add chopped fresh basil or any fresh herb and the dip becomes an excellent stuffing for tomatoes or on cucumbers. Use your imagination to come up with interesting variations.

Yield: 7 cups

1 pound frozen chopped spinach, thawed
2 cups sour cream
2 cups mayonnaise
1/2 teaspoon salt
1 tablespoon Worcestershire sauce
1 cup thinly sliced scallions
2 teaspoons minced garlic (optional)

Place spinach in a clean towel and squeeze out excess moisture. Transfer to a large bowl; combine with sour cream, mayonnaise, salt, Worcestershire, scallions and garlic, if desired.

Cover and chill until ready to serve.

Guacamole Grande

A great dip for tortilla chips with salsa.
Serve as a side with fajitas, enchiladas,
burritos or tacos. It also makes a good spread
on Veggie Burgers (page 132) or sandwiches.

Yield: 2 cups

4 ripe avocados
1/4 cup coarsely chopped fresh
   tomatoes
1/4 cup finely chopped onion
1 teaspoon minced garlic
1/2 cup chopped fresh cilantro,
   packed
1 tablespoon canned chopped
   jalapeños, drained
1 tablespoon lemon juice
1/4 teaspoon Tabasco sauce
1 teaspoon salt
2 tablespoons toasted pepitas
   (pumpkin seeds) or toasted
   sunflower seeds (page 12)
   (optional)

Cut avocado in half around seed and twist to free halves. Tap seed with large knife, hard enough so that seed sticks to knife. Twist knife causing seed to pop out of avocado. Tap knife on counter to remove seed; reserve seed. Scoop out avocado flesh and place in a small bowl. Mash flesh using fork or potato masher.

In a medium bowl, add tomatoes, onion, garlic, cilantro, jalapeños, lemon juice, Tabasco and 1 teaspoon salt or to taste; mix well. Garnish with a sprinkle of toasted pepitas. (This recipe may be prepared up to 2 hours in advance and refrigerated. Place reserved seed in guacamole to prevent color from darkening.)

Chapter 4

Salsas, Spreads and Sauces

Sensational Salsas

We love salsas at The Cheese Factory; hence the necessity to say a little something about their unique and versatile characteristics.

Along with its traditional role as a companion to Mexican dishes, the world of salsas encompasses a broad range of flavors, textures and colors that easily lend themselves to the spontaneous creation of inventive concoctions.

Salsa recipes need not be perfectly precise—anything can be converted to a salsa. For example: Cactus Salad (page 80), Bengali Cauliflower Curry (page 74), Cantaloupe and Tomato Salad with Avocado (page 83) or Cwikta—Beet and Horseradish Salad (page 73) are perfect salsa candidates. Simply reduce liquids and chop ingredients to desired chunkiness. Experiment with elements that you may have on hand including peppers, nuts, seeds, assorted fruits, vegetables and herbs.

Most salsas can be enhanced with sour cream, mayonnaise, yogurt or cheese sauce to add creamy richness to intensely stimulating flavors. Free-spirited salsa innovations make great snack or party food served with tortilla chips, toasted pita or focaccia bread. A salsa may be incorporated into any meal as an appetizer, dip, sauce or condiment and can be an ideal way to draw the elements of a dish together.

Tulsa Salsa

Personal taste plays a part in the creation of any recipe, and in this book the chipotle, a smoked chili pepper, will be found in abundance. It is available in two forms: dried, and canned in adobo sauce, a spicy tomato garlic sauce. The foundation of this excellent salsa recipe resides in the collaboration of chipotle, fresh cilantro and roasted cumin. The salsa keeps extremely well for one month in the refrigerator and freezes beautifully.

Yield: 1 quart salsa

 1 dried chipotle pepper,*
   stem removed
24 ounces (3 cups) canned diced
   tomatoes, drained
1/2 cup finely chopped onions
1/2 cup chopped fresh cilantro,
   packed
   Juice of 1 lime
 1 tablespoon minced garlic
 2 tablespoons canned chopped
   jalapeños
 1 tablespoon jalapeño juice
 1 tablespoon ground roasted
   cumin (page 13)
1/2 tablespoon chili powder
1/2 tablespoon salt
 1 teaspoon ground black pepper
 2 tablespoons brown sugar
1/8 teaspoon cayenne pepper

Reconstitute dried chipotle pepper in 1/2 cup hot water until softened. Drain and discard water. Finely chop pepper.

Combine chipotle pepper, tomatoes, onions, cilantro, lime juice, garlic, jalapeños, jalapeño juice, cumin, chili powder, salt, black pepper, brown sugar and cayenne in a medium bowl; mix well. Refrigerate until ready to serve.

*Available in Hispanic markets.

Tomatillo Salsa Verde

Native to Mexico and the southern United States, the small tart and pungent tomatillo is a green tomato (not an unripe tomato) used extensively in Mexican cooking. It is the key ingredient in this invigorating green salsa destined to ignite the fires of unsuspecting palates— a caution to more mild mannered taste buds.

Yield: 3 quarts salsa

   4 pounds fresh tomatillos*
   1 cup diced red peppers
1 1/2 cups finely chopped onions
   8 ounces (1 cup) canned chopped
      jalapeño peppers
 1/2 cup minced garlic
      Juice of 4 limes (3/4 cup)
 1/2 cup chopped fresh cilantro
   3 tablespoons salt
   4 tablespoons sugar
   1 cup white wine vinegar
   1 cup water
   2 tablespoons roasted ground
      cumin (page 13)
   2 teaspoons dried oregano,
      crumbled
1 1/2 teaspoons cayenne pepper

Remove tissue paper-like skin from tomatillos. Bring a large pot of water to boil and add tomatillos; blanch 2 minutes. Drain and immerse tomatillos in ice water to stop cooking; drain again. Purée half the tomatillos in a food processor and coarsely chop remaining half; place in a large bowl. Add red peppers, onions, jalapeños, garlic, lime juice, cilantro, salt, sugar, vinegar, water, cumin, oregano and cayenne; mix well. Refrigerate until ready to serve.

*Available in Hispanic markets.

Charbroiled Corn and Zucchini Salsa

This salsa is a blend of mild, slightly smoky flavors and crunchy textures
enveloped in a creamy garlic dressing and infused with the delicate fragrance
of fresh dill; it contains no hot chili peppers. It easily converts to a convincing
appetizer or salad when served in a nest of crisp greens. Add chilled
cooked potatoes for a brand new potato salad idea.
This recipe keeps well in the refrigerator for six days.

Yield: 3 quarts salsa

1 pound frozen corn kernels, thawed
   or 3 ears fresh corn on the cob
3 pounds zucchini
1 cup diced red pepper
1 cup finely chopped onions
2 tablespoons minced garlic
   Juice of 2 limes
2 cups mayonnaise
1 tablespoon dried dill, crumbled
1 tablespoon salt

If using frozen corn, heat 2 tablespoons olive oil in a large skillet and sear or lightly brown corn.

If using fresh corn on the cob, grill under a broiler or over hot coals, rotating ears until lightly charred. Cool and cut kernels from cobs.

Purée half the zucchini in a food processor and coarsely chop remaining half; place in a large bowl.

Add corn, red pepper, onions, garlic, lime juice, mayonnaise, dill and salt; mix well. Refrigerate until ready to serve.

Gingered Pineapple Salsa with Toasted Coconut

A culmination of tropically scented flavors and juicy, lush textures with just the right amount of sting. This salsa keeps well in the refrigerator for two weeks.

Yield: 2 quarts salsa

1 can (20 ounces) pineapple chunks in natural juice
1 can (20 ounces) crushed pineapple in natural juice
1 cup toasted coconut
1 cup thinly sliced scallions (green part only)
1/4 cup seeded and chopped fresh jalapeños
1 1/2 tablespoons minced fresh gingerroot
1/2 cup water
1/2 cup sugar
1 tablespoon salt
Zest and juice of 2 lemons
1/2 cup chopped fresh cilantro

In a large bowl, combine pineapple chunks, crushed pineapple, pineapple juice, coconut, scallions, jalapeños, gingerroot, water, sugar, salt, lemon zest, juice and cilantro. Mix well and refrigerate until ready to serve.

Sweet and Sassy Salsa

*Complement hot Mexican dishes, such as Chili Rellenos (page 149),
with this mildly spicy, tangy, sweet sauce. It has a refrigerated shelf life
of two weeks in the refrigerator and freezes well.*

Yield: 3 1/2 cups salsa

24 ounces (3 cups) canned diced
    plum tomatoes with juice
1/2 teaspoon ground fennel
1/2 teaspoon ground coriander
1/2 teaspoon ground white pepper
1 teaspoon roasted ground cumin
    (page 13)
1 1/2 teaspoons salt
1/8 teaspoon cayenne pepper
1 tablespoon fresh lemon juice
1 teaspoon minced garlic
1 tablespoon chili powder
1/4 cup brown sugar
1/2 cup chopped fresh cilantro,
    packed

In a medium bowl, combine tomatoes, fennel, coriander, white pepper, cumin, salt, cayenne, lemon juice, garlic, chili powder, brown sugar and cilantro; mix well. Refrigerate until ready to serve.

Cranberry Relish

*A new twist on an old favorite, this traditional holiday condiment
makes a great gift. It has a refrigerated shelf life of several weeks and
freezes beautifully. Try it on a bagel with cream cheese or on a freshly
baked muffin with lots of butter.*

Yield: 1 quart relish

4 oranges (reserve zest of 1 orange) 1/2 cup orange juice 1 pound whole fresh cranberries 11/2 cups sugar 2 whole garlic cloves 1 tablespoon Worcestershire sauce 1/2 teaspoon Tabasco sauce 3 tablespoons minced fresh gingerroot 2 teaspoons curry powder 2 cinnamon sticks 1/2 cup raisins	**Peel** and separate orange sections; set aside. **In** a heavy-bottomed 2-quart saucepan; combine orange juice, cranberries, sugar, garlic, Worcestershire, Tabasco, gingerroot, curry powder, cinnamon sticks and raisins. Bring to a gentle boil over medium heat; simmer 8 to 10 minutes. Remove garlic and cinnamon sticks. Stir in orange sections and zest; remove from heat and cool. Refrigerate until ready to serve.

Note: Stick garlic cloves on toothpicks for easy removal.

Scallion Cheese Spread

Delicious on a bagel,
in an omelette or as a sandwich filling,
this spread makes a great stuffing
for tomatoes or cucumbers.

Yield: 2³/4 cups cheese spread

2 packages (8 ounces each)
    cream cheese, softened
1/2 pound feta cheese, crumbled
3/4 cup thinly sliced scallions

Blend cream cheese, feta and scallions in a medium bowl with electric mixer on high speed. Chill 1 hour in refrigerator before serving.

Note: Using a food processor to combine ingredients will result in a looser consistency not suitable for a spread, but good as a dip.

Fresh Herb Cheese Spread

This spread is heavenly on sandwiches,
bagels, crackers, corn tortilla chips
and Cheese Factory Corn Bread (page 112).
It keeps well in the refrigerator for four days.

Yield: 1½ cups

1 package (8 ounces) cream
   cheese, softened
4 ounces sour cream
1 cup chopped fresh cilantro or
   dill, basil or Italian parsley

Combine cream cheese, sour cream and herbs in a medium bowl with electric mixer on high speed; mix well. Chill 1 hour in refrigerator before serving.

Note: A combination of herbs can be substituted for the cilantro.

Using a food processor to combine ingredients will result in a looser consistency not suitable for a spread, but good as a dip.

Basil Pesto

This rich, aromatic paste of Italian origin is traditionally made with fresh basil, garlic, pine nuts or walnuts, romano or Parmesan cheeses and virgin olive oil. For best results, use high-quality olive oil and imported cheeses. Lavish this sauce on pizza, sandwiches, pastas, vegetables or add to soups and stews to brighten flavors. It keeps well in the refrigerator for two weeks and freezes perfectly.

Yield: 1 cup pesto

1/2 cup toasted pine nuts or walnuts (page 12)
1 cup tightly packed fresh basil leaves
2 large garlic cloves, peeled
1/2 cup good-quality virgin olive oil
1/2 cup freshly grated imported Parmesan cheese
2 tablespoons freshly grated imported romano cheese
1 teaspoon salt
Freshly ground black pepper

Combine pine nuts, basil and garlic in a food processor. With the motor running, slowly add oil in a steady stream and process until smooth. Add Parmesan, romano, 1 teaspoon salt or to taste and pepper, as desired; process to incorporate ingredients. Refrigerate until ready to serve or freeze for later use.

Cilantro Pesto

For an exceptional burrito, spread pesto on flour tortilla; add
Jack cheese and Spicy Black Beans (page 119); fold, heat and serve with salsa.
Pesto can also be used to flavor soups or sauces, as a dip or on pizza.
Toss with pastas, rice or vegetables to enhance flavors.
Pesto keeps two weeks in the refrigerator and freezes well.

Yield: 2 cups pesto

1/4 cup slivered toasted almonds
    (page 12)
1 tablespoon minced garlic
1 cup olive oil
2 ounces feta cheese
2 cups fresh cilantro leaves, rinsed,
    patted dry and tightly packed
1 tablespoon lemon juice
1 teaspoon salt

Combine nuts, garlic, oil and feta in a food processor using metal blade attachment. Process until smooth; add cilantro, lemon juice and 1 teaspoon salt or to taste. Continue processing, scraping down sides as necessary until mixture is incorporated and smooth. Cover and refrigerate until ready to serve.

Kalamata Olive Pesto

Savor this pesto on toasted Italian bread, sandwiches or pizza.
Use as a dip for vegetables or spread on a cracker
and top with feta cheese.

Yield: 1 1/4 cups pesto

2 cups (12 ounces) kalamata olives,
    drained and pitted
2 tablespoons olive oil
2 tablespoons lemon juice
1/2 tablespoon minced garlic
1/2 teaspoon dried oregano, crumbled

Combine olives, oil, lemon juice, garlic and oregano in a food processor; process until smooth.

Sundried Tomato Pesto

This pesto is ideal served as a spread on pizza, crostini or focaccia.
Try it on a slice of sourdough bread with Brie or chèvre, fresh basil and
kalamata olives. For a delicious hot or cold side dish or entrée, toss with pasta,
rice or gnocchi dí patate. Keeps in the refrigerator two weeks and freezes well.

Yield: 2 cups pesto

7 1/2 ounces sundried tomatoes
      (2 cups)
  2 cups water
  1 tablespoon minced garlic
  1 cup olive oil
  1 tablespoon lemon juice
    Salt

Combine tomatoes and water in a 4-quart saucepan; bring to a boil. Reduce heat and simmer 5 minutes or until tomatoes are softened. Drain tomatoes, reserving liquid for soup stock or sauces, as desired.

Combine softened tomatoes, garlic, oil and lemon juice in food processor. Purée until smooth using steel blade attachment. Adjust seasoning with salt, as desired. For a looser consistency, add a little of the reserved tomato water. Refrigerate until ready to serve.

Cucumber Yogurt Sauce

*For those watching their weight, here is a simple, low-calorie sauce
that enhances the flavor of salad greens, vegetables and potatoes.
Excellent with falafel, this recipe harmonizes beautifully with Sfeeha
(Syrian Meat Pies, page 20). For a new flavor, substitute any herb for the
mint including fresh basil, fresh Italian parsley or dill.
Keeps well in the refrigerator for three days.*

Yield: 2 cups sauce

1 tablespoon cornstarch
1 quart plain low-fat yogurt
1 large cucumber (8 ounces)
   peeled, seeded and shredded
   Zest of 1 lemon
   Juice of 1/2 lemon
1 tablespoon minced garlic
2 tablespoons freshly chopped
   mint, packed, or 2 teaspoons
   dried mint, crumbled
1 teaspoon salt

Combine cornstarch and yogurt in a small bowl; whisk until well blended. Add cucumber, lemon zest and juice, garlic, mint and salt; mix well. Refrigerate until ready to serve.

Alfredo Sauce with Fresh Herbs

*Tasty on any kind of pasta, this sauce is scrumptious with
vegetables, such as mushrooms, asparagus, cauliflower or broccoli.
Prepare a casserole of scalloped potatoes using the Alfredo
between layers or serve as a topping over your favorite crêpes.*

Yield: 2 cups sauce

2 cups heavy cream
5 tablespoons butter
3/4 teaspoon salt
1/2 teaspoon grated nutmeg
1/8 teaspoon cayenne pepper
1/2 cup grated Parmesan
1 cup finely chopped fresh basil,
    Italian parsley, chives or mint
Freshly ground black pepper

Combine cream, butter, salt, nutmeg and cayenne in a heavy-bottomed 2-quart saucepan. Simmer (do not boil) 15 minutes or until sauce is slightly thickened.

Whisk in Parmesan and fresh herbs; simmer for another 5 minutes. Adjust seasonings with additional salt and pepper, as desired.

Country Gravy

Lavish this velvety smooth and richly seasoned gravy on mashed potatoes, Savory Corn Bread Dressing (page 113) or Festive Seitan Turkey (page 123); smother Homestyle Meatballs (page 128) or Meat Loaf (page 129) in it for savory sublime satisfaction. It can be made a day or two ahead and reheated. It keeps well refrigerated for four days.

Yield: 1 quart gravy

3 tablespoons vegetarian chicken-flavored powder
5 cups boiling water
1 cup half-and-half
1 small onion, peeled and quartered
2 whole garlic cloves, peeled
2 bay leaves
4 tablespoons butter
1/2 cup flour
1 teaspoon chopped fresh sage, or 1/4 teaspoon dried, crumbled
1 teaspoon chopped fresh rosemary, or 1/4 teaspoon dried, ground
1 teaspoon chopped fresh thyme, or 1/4 teaspoon dried, crumbled
1 teaspoon chopped fresh marjoram, or 1/4 teaspoon dried, crumbled
1 teaspoon Worcestershire sauce
1/2 teaspoon ground white pepper
Salt

Combine vegetarian chicken-flavored powder and boiling water in a small saucepan; add half-and-half, onion, garlic and bay leaves. Bring to a slow boil over medium heat; set aside.

Heat butter in another saucepan; add flour. Combine and stir with a wooden spoon over medium heat until flour begins to brown creating a dark, golden colored roux.

Strain vegetarian broth mixture through a sieve; add to roux. Whisk to incorporate ingredients.

Return bay leaves to saucepan; discard remaining ingredients in sieve. (If using dried herbs, add now.) Simmer 10 to 15 minutes over medium-low heat; whisk frequently until sauce is reduced to 4 cups. Add Worcestershire and pepper. (If using fresh herbs, add now.) Adjust seasonings with additional salt, as desired.

Mustard Sauce

Quick and easy to prepare, this recipe is a winner on almost any kind of
salad or vegetable. Mixed with a little mayonnaise, it makes a delicious
dressing for a potato salad or mixed bean salad. It's particularly good with
Seitan Pastrami (page 126) and Autumn Harvest Medley (page 100).
Serve it as a condiment along with the Barbecue Sauce (page 57)
on a charbroiled Veggie Burger (page 132).
Keeps well in the refrigerator for several weeks.

Yield: 1½ cups sauce

1 cup prepared dark or yellow
    mustard
1 tablespoon plus 1 teaspoon
    dry mustard
6 tablespoons sugar
5 tablespoons red wine or
    raspberry vinegar
1 cup olive oil
4 tablespoons freshly chopped dill,
    or 2 teaspoons dried,
    crumbled

Combine prepared and dry mustards, sugar and vinegar in a small bowl. Slowly whisk in oil to incorporate ingredients. When sauce is smooth, add dill and mix. Refrigerate 1 hour before serving.

Hot Orange Sauce

*This fragrant, spicy, sweet sauce interacts perfectly with many foods.
We've added it to cream sauces, stews, soups and salsas and served it
on squash, sweet potatoes, plantains and Cheese Factory Corn Bread (page 112).
It's been used as a glaze on Meat Loaf (page 129) and brushed on barbecued
vegetables. Experiment with new ideas for leftovers. There are no rules
for this; anything goes. The sauce keeps well in the refrigerator
for one month and freezes perfectly.*

Yield: 2 cups sauce

Zest of 2 oranges
Juice of 4 oranges
1 teaspoon minced fresh gingerroot
1 teaspoon minced garlic
2 tablespoons orange marmalade
1/4 cup packed brown sugar
1/2 teaspoon salt
1/4 teaspoon ground black pepper
1/2 teaspoon soy sauce
24 dried whole pequin chilis*
1 tablespoon cornstarch
1/2 cup cold water

Combine orange zest and juice, gingerroot, garlic, marmalade, brown sugar, salt, pepper, soy sauce and chilis in a 2-quart saucepan; place over medium heat. Dissolve cornstarch in cold water and add to saucepan. Cook over medium heat until sauce thickens slightly.

Note: Pequin chilis are about the size and shape of a navy bean.

*Available in Hispanic markets.

No Known Survivors

*As its name implies, this sauce is for "hot heads" only. Use it to spice up
Adios Gringos Chili (page 134), salsa or any dish you may want to "heat" up.
Keeps well in the refrigerator for two weeks and freezes perfectly.*

Yield: 2 cups sauce

1/4 cup dry mustard
2 tablespoons hot water
2 cans (7 ounces each) chipotle
   peppers in adobo sauce*
   Zest and juice of 1 orange
1/2 tablespoon salt
2 tablespoons roasted ground
   cumin (page 13)
1/2 tablespoon cayenne pepper
1/4 cup packed brown sugar
1/2 cup white wine vinegar

In a blender, combine mustard, hot water, chipotle peppers in sauce, orange zest and juice, salt, cumin, cayenne, brown sugar and vinegar; purée until smooth. Refrigerate until ready to serve or freeze for later use.

Note: For best results, we use the San Marcos brand of chipotle peppers in adobo sauce.

*Available in Hispanic markets.

Romesco Sauce

*Here's an adaptation of the classic Spanish romesco sauce traditionally made
with roasted peppers, chilis, garlic, olive oil and almonds. In Spain, this sauce
accompanies almost everything including meat, fish, fowl, vegetables and, of
course, the Tortilla Española (page 32). There is a standing joke among the
cooks at the restaurant that refers to the Romesco Sauce as being so versatile
and delicious that it could make cardboard taste good. What more can be said?
It keeps well in the refrigerator for five days and freezes perfectly.*

Yield: 2 cups sauce

1 can (12 ounces) pimientos, drained,
   or 1/2 recipe (3 Roasted Red
   Peppers, page 16), unmarinated
2 1/2 ounces slivered toasted almonds
   (page 12)
2 teaspoons minced garlic
1 1/2 tablespoons chipotle in adobo sauce*
1/2 cup olive oil
1 1/2 tablespoons balsamic vinegar
1 1/2 teaspoons salt

Combine pimientos, almonds, garlic, chipotle peppers in sauce, oil, vinegar and salt in blender; purée until smooth.

Note: For best results, we use the San Marcos brand of chipotle peppers in adobo sauce.

*Available in Hispanic markets.

Barbecue Sauce

*This is a no-cook barbecue sauce, great on tofu, tempeh, seitan,
meatballs and meat loaf. We use it to marinate vegetables before charbroiling
(page 102) and to enhance the flavor of baked beans, soups, sauces and dips.
Western Spice is a handy blend to have in the pantry. Add it to salad
dressings, grilled vegetables, beans, soups, stews or rice.
The Barbecue Sauce keeps well in the refrigerator
for one month and freezes perfectly.*

Yield: 3 cups Barbecue Sauce

1 cup Western Spice

Western Spice:
- 1 tablespoon dried oregano, crumbled
- 1 tablespoon dried thyme, crumbled
- 1 tablespoon onion powder
- 1 tablespoon ground black pepper
- 1 tablespoon ground white pepper
- 2 tablespoons cayenne pepper
- 2 tablespoons ground fennel
- 3 tablespoons paprika
- 3 tablespoons garlic powder

Barbecue Sauce:
- 2 tablespoons Western Spice
- 1 can (7 ounces) chipotle peppers in adobo sauce*
- 1/2 cup finely chopped onions
- 2 teaspoons minced garlic
- 2 teaspoons minced fresh gingerroot
- Zest and juice of 1/2 orange
- Juice of 1/2 lemon
- 2 cups catsup
- 2 tablespoons prepared mustard
- 1 tablespoon liquid hickory smoke
- 1 tablespoon Worcestershire sauce
- 3/4 cup packed brown sugar
- 1 teaspoon salt
- 1/4 teaspoon ground cloves

To make Western Spice, combine oregano, thyme, onion powder, black pepper, white pepper, cayenne, fennel, paprika and garlic powder in a small bowl. Store in a sealed container.

Purée chipotle peppers in adobo sauce in blender. Reserve 2 tablespoons for Barbecue Sauce and refrigerate or freeze the rest for later use. (Keeps for several weeks in refrigerator.)

Combine Western Spice, 2 tablespoons reserved puréed chipotle peppers in sauce, onions, garlic, gingerroot, orange zest and juice, lemon juice, catsup, mustard, liquid smoke, Worcestershire, brown sugar, salt and cloves in a small bowl; mix well. Refrigerate until ready to serve or freeze for later use.

Note: For best results, we use the San Marcos brand of chipotle peppers in adobo sauce.

*Available in Hispanic markets.

Marinara Sauce

This full-bodied, aromatic tomato sauce deviates a little from the traditional Italian version which never includes cheese. Serve it on pasta with Homestyle Meatballs (page 128) or mix with Italian Crumble Sausage (page 133) for a great Italian-style meat sauce. Keeps well in the refrigerator for one week and freezes perfectly.

Yield: 2 quarts sauce

2 tablespoons olive oil
1/2 cup finely chopped onion
2 teaspoons minced garlic
1/4 cup finely chopped celery
1/4 cup finely chopped green pepper
1 teaspoon whole fennel seeds
1/4 teaspoon hot pepper flakes
1 can (29 ounces) tomato sauce
1 can (14 1/2 ounces) peeled Italian plum tomatoes with juice, coarsely chopped
1 can (8 ounces) tomato juice
1 can (6 ounces) tomato paste
1 teaspoon salt
1 teaspoon dried basil, crumbled
1/4 teaspoon dried thyme, crumbled
1/2 teaspoon dried oregano, crumbled
1/2 teaspoon ground fennel
1/4 teaspoon coarsely ground black pepper
2 tablespoons sugar
2 bay leaves
1 tablespoon chopped fresh Italian parsley
1/2 cup grated Parmesan

Heat oil in a heavy-bottomed 5-quart saucepan. Add onion, garlic, celery, green pepper, fennel seeds and hot pepper flakes; sauté 3 to 5 minutes. Add tomato sauce, tomatoes, tomato juice, tomato paste, salt, basil, thyme, oregano, fennel, pepper, sugar, bay leaves, parsley and cheese. Bring to a slow boil and simmer approximately 45 minutes, stirring frequently.

Chapter 5

Soups

Mushroom Barley Soup

This interpretation of an old favorite features shiitake mushrooms and texturized vegetable protein to create a hearty, beefy soup that may be served as a main course with crusty bread and a salad. The soup freezes well and has a refrigerated shelf life of one week.

Yield: 4 quarts

24 dried shiitake mushrooms*
     (1 1/2 ounces), stems removed
     and discarded
2 cups boiling water
2 tablespoons olive oil
2 cups diced onion
2 teaspoons minced garlic
1 cup diced carrots
1/2 cup diced celery
4 roma tomatoes (3/4 pound),
     coarsely chopped (2 cups)
1 teaspoon dried thyme, crumbled
1/2 cup soy sauce
3 quarts water
1 cup pearl barley, uncooked
2 bay leaves
1 cup texturized vegetable
     protein** (TVP) (page 5)
2 teaspoons salt
1 teaspoon freshly ground
     black pepper
1 tablespoon Worcestershire sauce
1/4 cup chopped fresh Italian
     parsley, packed

Soak shiitakes in boiling water for 20 minutes. Drain; reserving water for soup. Thinly slice shiitakes; set aside.

Heat oil in a 5-quart soup pot; add onion and garlic. Sauté until onion turns translucent; add carrots and celery. Cook over medium heat until lightly caramelized. Add chopped tomato and cook 1 minute. Add thyme, shiitakes, reserved shiitake water, soy sauce and 3 quarts water. Bring to a boil over high heat; add barley and bay leaves. Cover; simmer gently 45 minutes to 1 hour or until barley is plump and tender. Add TVP and cook 5 minutes more. Add 2 teaspoons salt or to taste, 1 teaspoon black pepper or to taste and Worcestershire. Garnish with freshly chopped Italian parsley.

*Available in Oriental markets.
**Available in natural food markets.

Carrot Ginger Soup

*Try this blazing autumn-hued soup using butternut squash or sweet potatoes
instead of carrots. Adorn each serving with a variety of interesting garnishes,
such as toasted coconut, toasted pumpkin or sesame seeds, thinly julienned
carrots, paper-thin slices of peeled orange or a sprig of fresh mint.*

Yield: 2½ quarts

3/4	pound potatoes, peeled and coarsely chopped (2 cups)
3	tablespoons butter
1	cup chopped onion
1	tablespoon minced fresh gingerroot
2¼	pounds carrots, peeled and coarsely chopped (6 cups)
2	tablespoons vegetarian chicken-flavored powder
3	cups boiling water
4 to 5	cups water
1/8	teaspoon ground mace
1/8	teaspoon ground cardamom
1/2	cup half-and-half (optional)
1¼	teaspoons salt
1/4	teaspoon ground white pepper

Immerse potatoes in cold water; set aside.

Heat butter in a 5-quart soup pot; add onion, gingerroot and carrots. Sauté 2 to 3 minutes over medium-high heat.

Prepare broth by dissolving vegetarian chicken-flavored powder in boiling water. Drain potatoes and add vegetarian broth and potatoes to vegetable mixture. Cover and bring to a boil. Reduce heat; simmer 15 to 20 minutes or until vegetables are tender.

Place vegetables in blender and purée until smooth. Return to saucepan; add 4 to 5 cups water (or to desired consistency). Gently reheat over medium heat; add mace, cardamom and half-and-half. (Do not allow to boil.) Adjust seasonings with salt and pepper, as desired.

Hot and Sour Soup

The robust authentic flavor of this soup is a favorite among staff and guests alike. Prepare an Oriental dinner deemed worthy of your favorite Chinese restaurant—include the soup, Egg Rolls with Apricot Ginger Sauce (page 24) and Oriental Stir-Fry with Tamarind Ginger Garlic Sauce (page 160).

Yield: 2 1/2 quarts

 1 dried wood ear mushroom*
12 dried shiitake mushrooms,*
    stems removed and discarded
 1 quart boiling water
 2 tablespoons vegetable shortening
1/2 cup thinly sliced onion
1/2 cup thinly sliced celery,
    cut on the diagonal
 1 tablespoon minced garlic
1/2 cup vegetarian chicken-flavored
    powder
 1 quart boiling water
1/2 teaspoon cayenne pepper
 6 tablespoons soy sauce
2/3 cup rice vinegar
 1 teaspoon coarsely ground
    black pepper
 2 dried hot Chinese peppers*
 6 tablespoons cornstarch
2/3 cup cold water
 4 ounces tofu, soft or firm
    (1/4-inch dice)
 1 tablespoon dark sesame oil
 3 tablespoons thinly sliced scallions
 2 large eggs (optional)

*Available in Asian or Oriental markets.

Reconstitute dried mushrooms in boiling water for 20 minutes. Drain and reserve water. Thinly slice mushrooms; set aside.

Heat shortening in a 5-quart soup pot; add onion, celery and garlic. Sauté until onion is wilted. Prepare broth by dissolving vegetarian chicken-flavored powder in boiling water; stir into pot. Add mushrooms and reserved mushroom-flavored water to soup. Add cayenne, soy sauce, vinegar, black pepper and Chinese peppers. (For additional heat, crumble Chinese peppers into soup.) Bring to a boil over high heat.

Dissolve cornstarch and cold water in a small bowl; stir into soup. Return to a boil; reduce heat and simmer until soup begins to thicken. Add tofu and sesame oil. Remove from heat; garnish with scallions.

Optional: Break eggs into a small bowl; whisk briefly, using a fork. Pour eggs in a gentle stream from about 5 inches above soup while stirring egg ribbons throughout soup.

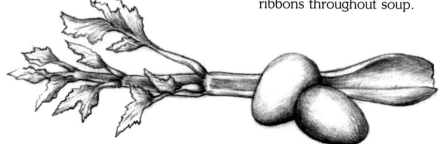

Wisconsin Beer Cheese Soup

Tourists find a way to enjoy Wisconsin beer and cheese together in this distinctive soup. The recipe readily converts to a zesty cheese sauce—reduce water by 1½ cups. Serve it as a sauce over baked potatoes, broccoli or cauliflower, as a topping on crêpes and pastas or as a dip for pretzels and chips. Although any beer will do, we recommend an authentic Wisconsin-brewed variety—Old Milwaukee.

Yield: 2½ quarts

3/4 cup (1½ sticks) butter
1 cup finely chopped onions
1 tablespoon minced garlic
1/2 cup finely chopped celery
1/2 cup finely chopped carrots
1/2 cup flour
1/4 cup vegetarian chicken-flavored powder
3 cups boiling water
1/2 cup beer
2 teaspoons Worcestershire sauce
2 cups whole milk
1/4 cup heavy cream
2 tablespoons sugar
2 teaspoons dry mustard
1/2 teaspoon ground fennel
1/8 teaspoon cayenne pepper
5 cups grated Wisconsin Cheddar cheese

Heat butter in a heavy 5-quart soup pot; add onions and garlic. Sauté until onions are translucent; add celery and carrots. Cook 2 to 3 minutes; stir in flour. Prepare broth by dissolving vegetarian chicken-flavored powder in boiling water. Add to soup and bring to a boil over high heat. Add beer, Worcestershire, milk and cream. Reduce heat to low; simmer 5 minutes. Add sugar, mustard, fennel and cayenne; cook 1 minute longer. Add cheese, stirring constantly until cheese is melted and soup begins to bubble.

If soup seems a little too thick, add additional vegetarian broth or warm milk, as desired; remove from heat. Garnish with a sprinkle of paprika.

Split Pea Soup
with Smoked Seitan

*Dried beans have traditionally had a reputation as peasant fare,
perhaps due to their dominant role in the diet of poor folk the world over.
There is nothing humble about this rustic combination of ingredients.
Split peas absorb the complex and subtle flavors of the aromatic vegetables
and smoky seitan, which results in a hearty, comforting winter dish.
Serve with good crusty bread and cheese. This soup keeps in the
refrigerator for one week and freezes perfectly.*

Yield: 2 quarts

$1/2$ cup soy sauce
2 tablespoons liquid smoke
2 tablespoons sugar
6 ounces seitan, cut into
   $1/4$-inch-thick slices (page 122)
   or purchase prepared
   commercial seitan
2 tablespoons vegetable oil
1 cup finely chopped onion
1 teaspoon minced garlic
$1^1/2$ cups diced carrot ($1/4$-inch dice)
$1^1/2$ cups diced celery ($1/4$-inch dice)
3 tablespoons vegetarian chicken-
   flavored powder
2 quarts boiling water
2 bay leaves
$1^1/2$ cups split peas
   Salt and pepper
2 tablespoons chopped fresh
   Italian parsley

Combine soy sauce, liquid smoke and sugar in a small bowl; add seitan. Marinate 30 minutes. Drain seitan; cut into $1/4$-inch cubes. Freeze smoke marinade for later use.

Heat oil in a heavy-bottomed 4-quart soup pot. Add onion, garlic, carrot and celery. Sauté over high heat 2 to 3 minutes until onion turns translucent. Prepare broth by dissolving vegetarian chicken-flavored powder in boiling water; stir into soup. Add bay leaves and split peas; bring to a boil. Cover and simmer 40 minutes or until peas are tender. Add seitan and simmer an additional 5 minutes. Adjust seasonings with salt and pepper, as desired. Garnish with parsley.

Minestrone

*Indulge in a thick, hearty, savory soup that is a meal in itself.
There are dozens of variations on this Italian masterpiece. Explore infinite
creative possibilities, perhaps using this version as a guideline.
The soup keeps in the refrigerator for one week and freezes perfectly.*

Yield: 5 quarts

2 tablespoons olive oil
1 1/2 cups finely chopped onion
1 teaspoon minced garlic
1/4 cup diced celery
1 cup carrots, peeled and sliced
    into 1/8-inch-thick half-moons
1 1/2 cups sliced mushrooms
1 teaspoon dried oregano,
    crumbled
1 teaspoon dried basil, crumbled
1/4 teaspoon ground fennel
2 tablespoons vegetarian
    chicken-flavored powder
2 1/2 quarts boiling water
1 teaspoon A.1. steak sauce
1/2 teaspoon Worcestershire sauce
1 box (10 ounces) frozen
    chopped spinach, thawed
    and drained
1 can (28 ounces) crushed
    tomatoes
1 jar (28 ounces) Prego
    Traditional Spaghetti Sauce
1 can (28 ounces) kidney or
    navy beans, drained and
    rinsed
1 1/2 cups zucchini, cut into
    1/2-inch bite-size pieces
1 1/2 to 2 cups cooked Gnocchi di Patate
    (page 111) or any small-
    shaped cooked pasta
Salt and pepper
3 tablespoons Basil Pesto
    (page 47)
3 tablespoons good-quality
    grated Parmesan cheese

Heat oil in an 8-quart soup pot; add onion, garlic, celery and carrots. Sauté 2 to 3 minutes until onion turns translucent; add mushrooms, oregano, basil and fennel. Cook 1 to 2 minutes longer over medium heat until mushrooms soften. Prepare broth by dissolving vegetarian chicken-flavored powder in boiling water; stir into soup. Add steak sauce, Worcestershire, spinach, tomatoes, spaghetti sauce and beans; bring to a boil over high heat. Simmer 10 minutes; add zucchini and cook 5 minutes longer. Add gnocchi. Adjust seasonings with salt and pepper, as desired. Remove from heat.

Add pesto and Parmesan just before serving.

French Onion Soup

It is difficult to believe that there is not a single drop of beef stock in this soup. Full-bodied, richly flavored and subtly enhanced by the seasoned croutons and Swiss cheese, this soup is a welcome addition to a vegetarian soup repertoire.

Yield: 3 quarts soup

3 quarts croutons

Croutons:
- 4 tablespoons butter, melted
- 1/4 cup olive oil
- 1 tablespoon balsamic vinegar
- 2 tablespoons minced garlic
- 2 teaspoons dried basil, crumbled
- 2 teaspoons dried thyme, crumbled
- 1 tablespoon dried oregano, crumbled
- 2 teaspoons garlic powder
- 1 pound commercial croutons (1/2-inch cubes)
- 2 tablespoons grated romano

Soup:
- 1/2 cup (1 stick) butter
- 2 large Bermuda onions (1 1/2 pounds), peeled and thinly sliced (about 7 cups)
- 2 teaspoons sugar
- 6 tablespoons vegetarian beef-flavored powder or 6 tablespoons soy sauce
- 3 quarts boiling water
- 2 teaspoons dry sherry or cognac
- 2 teaspoons salt
- 1/2 teaspoon coarsely ground black pepper
- 8 slices (1 1/2 to 2 ounces each) Swiss cheese (we recommend Gruyère)
- 4 tablespoons good-quality freshly grated Parmesan cheese
- Paprika for garnish
- Chopped parsley for garnish

Preheat oven to 300 degrees F.

To make croutons, combine butter, oil, vinegar, garlic, basil, thyme, oregano and garlic powder in a small bowl; mix well. Transfer croutons to a large bowl; add herb mixture and sprinkle with romano. Mix using hands until croutons are coated evenly. Spread single layer of croutons in shallow baking pan; bake 3 to 5 minutes until crisp and crunchy. Cool and store in an airtight container up to 1 month. (Do not refrigerate.)

To make soup, heat butter in a 5-quart soup pot; add onions and sugar. Sauté over medium heat to caramelize onions. Prepare broth by dissolving vegetarian beef-flavored powder in boiling water; stir into soup. Cover and simmer 30 minutes. Add sherry. Remove from heat and adjust seasonings with salt and pepper, as desired.

To serve, place soup in individual baking crocks and top with 2/3 cup croutons and 1 slice Swiss cheese. Broil until cheese is melted and lightly browned. Sprinkle with Parmesan, paprika and parsley.

Zucchini Basil Soup

Bursting with color, this bright green soup has a smooth and velvety texture. You can expect the same results from a non-dairy variation—just substitute olive oil for the butter. An alternative for dried basil is 4-5 tablespoons of fresh basil, chopped. Toasted pumpkin seeds sprinkled on top make a perfect garnish.

Yield: 2¹/₂ quarts

5 tablespoons butter
1 large onion (³/₄ pound),
    peeled and sliced
2 tablespoons dried basil, crumbled
¹/₄ cup vegetarian chicken-flavored
    powder
2 cups boiling water
5 cups water
1 large Idaho potato (³/₄ pound),
    peeled and chopped
2 teaspoons salt
6 large zucchini (2¹/₂ pounds),
    chopped
    Salt and freshly ground
    black pepper

Heat butter in a 5-quart soup pot; add onions and sauté until translucent. Add dried basil (if using fresh basil, add at the end); cook 30 seconds. Prepare broth by dissolving vegetarian chicken-flavored powder in boiling water; stir into soup. Add 3 cups of the water, potato and salt; bring to a boil. Reduce heat and simmer until potatoes are tender. Add zucchini and cook 5 minutes. Remove from heat. (The bright green color is key to this soup, so do not overcook zucchini.) Allow soup to cool slightly; purée in blender until smooth.

Return soup to pot and add up to 2 cups remaining water for desired consistency. Reheat gently over medium heat; adjust seasonings with salt and pepper, as desired.

Borscht

*A stimulating soup from Russia, abounding in intense flavors,
may be served hot or cold or garnished with a dollop of sour cream.
A good loaf of hearty rye bread makes a perfect accompaniment.*

Yield: 3 quarts

  2 tablespoons vegetable oil
  1 cup thinly sliced onion
  2 teaspoons minced garlic
  3 cups shredded red cabbage
  1 cup diced carrots (1/4-inch)
3/4 cup vegetarian beef-flavored
       powder
  6 cups boiling water
  2 cans (15 ounces each) beets with
       juice, cut into 1/4-inch dice
1 1/2 teaspoons caraway seeds
  1 cup red wine vinegar
  2 tablespoons lemon juice
1/2 cup sugar
  1 teaspoon coarsely ground
       black pepper
  1 teaspoon salt
1/4 teaspoon cayenne pepper
       (optional)

Heat oil in a 5-quart sauce pot; add onions and garlic. Sauté until onion turns translucent. Add cabbage and carrots. Cover and cook 2 minutes over medium-high heat until cabbage is wilted. Make broth by dissolving vegetarian beef-flavored powder in boiling water; stir into soup and bring to a boil over high heat. Add beets, caraway seeds, vinegar, lemon juice, sugar, pepper, 1 teaspoon salt or to taste and cayenne; simmer 30 minutes or until vegetables are tender.

Variation: Omit vegetarian beef-flavored powder and water; replace with 3/4 cup soy sauce mixed with 5 1/4 cups water.

Wild Rice with Yams and Hominy Soup

Wild rice can be categorized as the truffle of the grain world.
Until about 1975 the grain remained wild and was harvested in Minnesota
and Wisconsin by Winnebago and Chippewa Indians. Today almost
half of all wild rice is farmed in paddy fields in California, Minnesota
and Wisconsin. However, because it is still difficult to produce in large
quantities, wild rice remains extremely expensive. Hominy, dried
and processed field corn, wild rice and yams are foods native to
North America. This recipe captures and releases their
individual characteristics in a distinctive composition.

Yield: 3 quarts

2 tablespoons olive oil
1 cup finely chopped onion
1 teaspoon minced garlic
1/2 cup diced celery
1 teaspoon dried thyme, crumbled
1 teaspoon dried marjoram, crumbled
1 teaspoon dried sage, crumbled
6 tablespoons vegetarian chicken-flavored powder
3 quarts boiling water
1 can (16 ounces) hominy, drained and rinsed (1 1/2 cups)
6 ounces wild rice (1 cup)
1 bay leaf
1 large yam (12 ounces), peeled, cut into 1/4-inch dice (2 cups)
1/2 cup frozen corn kernels, thawed
1/2 cup frozen green peas, thawed
1 small red pepper, seeded and diced
1 teaspoon ground black pepper
1/2 cup chopped fresh Italian parsley
Salt

Heat oil in a 5-quart sauce pot; add onion, garlic and celery. Sauté over high heat until onion turns translucent. Add thyme, marjoram and sage; cook 30 seconds. Prepare broth by dissolving vegetarian chicken-flavored powder in boiling water; stir into soup. Add hominy, rice and bay leaf; cover and bring to a boil.

Reduce heat and simmer 35 to 40 minutes. Add yams and cook an additional 10 minutes or until yams are tender. Add corn, peas, red pepper, black pepper and parsley. Adjust seasonings with additional salt, as desired.

Chilled Melon Soup

*Savor the rejuvenating quality of this refreshing fruit soup
with cantaloupe, cranshaw or honeydew. This soup is best served in summer
when melons are at their peak. The cream may be substituted with yogurt or
omitted altogether. The taste of the soup will vary based on the quality
of the melon. Adjust sugar, salt and lemon juice as necessary in order
to heighten or round out the flavors.*

Yield: 3 1/2 quarts

4 cantaloupes (11 pounds), peeled,
   seeded and cubed (about 4 1/2
   quarts)
2 1/2 teaspoons salt
2 1/2 tablespoons lemon juice
1/2 teaspoon nutmeg
   Zest of 1 orange
4 tablespoons heavy cream
   or yogurt
8 fresh strawberries for garnish
   Fresh mint for garnish

Combine melon, salt, lemon juice, nutmeg and orange zest in a blender; purée until smooth. Pour into a large bowl; add cream. Stir and chill at least 2 hours before serving.

Remove stems from strawberries and discard. Thinly slice strawberries. To serve, ladle soup into bowls; garnish with 3 to 4 strawberry slices and a sprig of mint.

Chapter 6

Salads and Salad Dressings

Chilled Asparagus with Sesame Vinaigrette

*The deep, rich flavor of the sesame dressing is an appealing
contrast to the lightness of the asparagus. Served warm or cold,
this vegetable salad makes a wonderful appetizer. Delicious with grains,
such as Quinoa with Fresh Cilantro (page 115) or wild rice,
it easily transforms into a no-fat, low-calorie dish
by eliminating or reducing the sesame oil.*

Yield: 8 servings

2 to 3 pounds fresh asparagus
          (16 to 18 spears per pound)
5 tablespoons dark sesame oil
2 1/2 tablespoons rice vinegar
2 1/2 tablespoons soy sauce or tamari
2 teaspoons sugar
   Salt and pepper
1/4 cup toasted sesame seeds
       (page 12)

Cut approximately 1 inch or more off the end of asparagus stalk and discard. Using a vegetable peeler, pare approximately 1 inch or so of the stalk to remove any remaining tough fibers. Steam or blanch asparagus in boiling water until crisp-tender. (The amount of time will vary depending on the size and thickness of the stalks.) Drain and immerse in ice water to chill. Drain; pat dry with paper towel and place in serving dish.

Mix oil, vinegar, soy sauce and sugar in a small bowl; adjust seasonings with salt and pepper, as desired. Pour over asparagus and marinate overnight in refrigerator.

Serve garnished with toasted sesame seeds.

Cwikta

(Beet and Horseradish Salad)

*This recipe was handed down to one of our cooks by her Polish grandmother
and is an appetizing way to enjoy canned beets. Offer it as a spicy, tangy
counterpoint to the creamy richness of Mushroom Potato Stroganoff (page 162)
or Tofu Chicken Paprikash (page 138). For a light luncheon or supper, serve it
with fresh, crispy greens, sliced hard-boiled eggs and boiled new potatoes.*

Yield: 5 1/2 cups

3 cans (15 ounces each) sliced beets,
    reserve 3/4 cup juice
1/4 cup grated horseradish
3/4 cup red wine vinegar
1 1/2 teaspoons salt
1/2 cup sugar
1 tablespoon caraway seeds

Drain beets; slice into matchsticks and place in a large bowl. Combine beet juice, horseradish, vinegar, salt, sugar and caraway seeds in a small bowl; pour over beets.

Chill at least 2 hours before serving. Serve with a dollop of sour cream.

Bengali Cauliflower Curry

A bright, light curry without the heat, this dish is redolent with the
fragrance of roasted spices, which satisfies that craving for Indian flavors.
Add marinated, deep-fried tofu (chicken-cut, page 3) and serve with
rice noodles or rice for a delicious light entrée. Tangy Acorn Squash (page 101),
Quinoa with Fresh Cilantro (page 115), Minted Couscous (page 117)
or lentils are several good choices to accompany this vegetable dish.

Yield: 3 quarts

Dressing:

2 teaspoons whole coriander seeds,*
   roasted and ground (page 13)
2 teaspoons whole roasted cumin
   seeds (page 13)
2 tablespoons minced fresh
   gingerroot
2 cups mayonnaise
4 tablespoons lemon juice
1 tablespoon plus 1 teaspoon curry
   powder
1 tablespoon minced garlic
1 teaspoon salt
1/4 teaspoon cayenne pepper
   (optional)

Vegetables:

3 quarts water
2 tablespoons salt
1 1/2 pounds cauliflower (trimmed),
   cut into flowerets (8 cups)
2 carrots (12 ounces), peeled;
   cut in half lengthwise and sliced
   on the diagonal into half-moons
   (3 cups)
2 cups frozen corn kernels, thawed
2 cups frozen green peas, thawed
1 cup finely diced red onion
2 1/2 ounces slivered toasted almonds
   (1/2 cup) (page 12)
   Salt and freshly ground
   black pepper

To make dressing, in a small bowl, combine coriander, cumin seeds, gingerroot, mayonnaise, lemon juice, curry powder, garlic, 1 teaspoon salt or to taste and cayenne; whisk to incorporate ingredients.

To make vegetables, bring water and salt to a boil in a 3-quart saucepan. Add cauliflower and carrots; cook 2 to 3 minutes. Drain and immerse vegetables in ice water to stop cooking. Vegetables should be crisp-tender; drain well.

Combine cauliflower, carrots, corn, peas, onions and almonds in a large bowl. Toss with dressing; adjust seasonings with salt and pepper, as desired. Marinate 2 hours in refrigerator before serving.

*Available in Asian markets.

Melidzanes Salata
(Greek Eggplant Salad)

The smoky, aromatic blend of charbroiled eggplant, fresh herbs, feta, Greek olives, tomatoes and peppers is an irresistible collaboration. Served on a bed of salad greens with toasted pita bread, this recipe makes a wonderful entrée on a hot summer day.

Yield: 2 quarts

2 eggplant (2 pounds)
2 teaspoons salt
2 tablespoons olive oil
2 green peppers (12 ounces), seeded and cut into 1/2-inch squares
3 roma tomatoes (10 ounces), cut into 1/2-inch bite-size pieces
3/4 cup finely diced red onion
1 cup pitted kalamata olives, quartered lengthwise
12 ounces feta cheese, cut into 1/2-inch cubes
1/2 cup chopped fresh Italian parsley, mint or basil

Dressing:
1 tablespoon minced garlic
2 tablespoons balsamic vinegar
2 tablespoons lemon juice
1/2 cup olive oil
1/4 teaspoon allspice
Salt and freshly ground black pepper

Cut stems and bottoms off eggplant and discard. Slice lengthwise into 3/4-inch-thick slabs; place on a rack over a shallow pan. Lightly salt both sides and allow to drain for 1 hour.

Rinse eggplant and pat dry. Brush both sides with oil; grill over hot coals or bake in a 400-degree F oven until tender (approximately 30 minutes). Remove from heat; cool to room temperature.

Cut eggplant into 1/2-inch bite-size chunks and place in a large bowl. Add peppers, tomatoes, onions, olives, feta and herbs.

To make dressing, combine garlic, vinegar, lemon juice, oil and allspice in a small bowl; toss with vegetables. Adjust seasonings with salt and pepper, as desired. Marinate 2 hours before serving.

Chilled Sesame Spinach

This recipe was discovered at a favorite Japanese restaurant in Madison, Wisconsin. Back at The Cheese Factory, it was adapted by one of our cooks and served as an accompaniment to the Norimaki with Vegetables (page 28). The sweet dressing interacts with the slightly bitter greens to create an interesting and delicious side dish, salad or appetizer.

Yield: 8 cups

3 pounds frozen whole leaf
spinach, thawed

Dressing:
1/2 cup sugar
1/2 cup tamari or soy sauce
1/2 cup dark sesame oil
1/2 cup toasted sesame seeds
(page 12)

Drain spinach; place in a clean towel and squeeze out excess moisture; transfer to a large bowl.

To make dressing, combine sugar, tamari and oil in a small bowl; stir until well blended.

Add dressing to spinach and lightly toss to coat. Shape into individual nests or mounds and sprinkle with sesame seeds.

Mostaccioli with Sundried Tomatoes and Capers

Mostaccioli is a hollow, tubular pasta cut obliquely, about 2½ inches long. Any pasta shape may be substituted for the mostaccioli, but the dark, mellow, subtle, sweet flavor of balsamic vinegar is an essential ingredient in this recipe. Also featured are capers, the pickled flower buds of the caper plant, a prickly shrub found in the Mediterranean region. These fragrant little bursts of flavor are sensational in cold or hot pasta, on pizza or in sandwiches.

Yield: 3 quarts

4 ounces sundried tomatoes (1 cup)

Dressing:
1/2 cup balsamic vinegar
3/4 cup olive oil
1 tablespoon minced garlic
1/2 cup chopped fresh Italian parsley
1/2 cup thinly sliced scallions

1 pound dry mostaccioli,
 cooked al dente
1 jar (3 ounces) capers,
 brine reserved
1/2 cup toasted walnuts, pine nuts
 or slivered almonds (page 12)
1/2 teaspoon salt
1 teaspoon freshly ground
 black pepper

Reconstitute sundried tomatoes in 2 cups hot water for 20 minutes. Drain; reserve water for soup or stock, if desired. Cut tomatoes lengthwise into 1/4-inch-thick slices.

To make dressing, combine vinegar, oil, garlic, parsley and scallions in a small bowl; whisk to incorporate ingredients.

Combine pasta, tomatoes, dressing, 3 tablespoons drained capers, 3 tablespoons reserved brine, nuts, 1/2 teaspoon salt or to taste and pepper in a large bowl; toss well. Serve immediately or chill until ready to use.

Tempeh Tuna Salad

This delicious alternative to tuna salad may be served on a bed of greens or in a sandwich. Use it to stuff a variety of vegetables including tomatoes, zucchini and cucumbers. Try substituting it for the chicken salad in the Lettuce Bundles (page 19). Some of our cooks like to include diced apple or pickle relish instead of the diced dill pickle. Use low-fat or no-fat mayonnaise in the dressing to provide a tasty, low-calorie appetizer, side dish or salad.

Yield: 6 cups

2 packages (8 ounces each)
  sea veggie tempeh or original
  soy tempeh* (page 5)
1 teaspoon salt
1 cup toasted walnuts or cashews
  (page 12)
1 cup diced celery
1/2 cup finely chopped red onion
1 cup diced dill pickle
1 cup chopped fresh Italian parsley

Dressing:
1 1/2 cups mayonnaise
1 tablespoon minced garlic
2 tablespoons lemon juice
2 tablespoons Worcestershire sauce
2 teaspoons dried oregano,
  crumbled
1 teaspoon freshly ground
  black pepper
1 tablespoon prepared mustard
1 teaspoon salt

Cut tempeh into 1/2-inch cubes; sprinkle with salt and place in a steamer for 20 minutes. Set aside and cool to room temperature.

In a medium bowl, combine tempeh, nuts, celery, onion, pickle and parsley.

To make dressing, combine mayonnaise, garlic, lemon juice, Worcestershire, oregano, pepper, mustard and 1 teaspoon salt or to taste in a separate bowl; mix thoroughly. Add to tempeh mixture. Toss, cover and chill for 2 hours before serving.

*Available in natural food markets.

Mexican "Ouchies"

Wondering about the name of this recipe? Allow us to enlighten you.
Those jalapeño peppers are the culprits and exclamations of "ouch, ouch, ouch"
have been overheard while chomping down on those spicy, South-of-the-Border
marinated vegetables. To cut the heat, simply use less jalapeños. A perfect
complement to any of our Mexican dishes, this salad should be prepared
several days in advance for full maturation of flavors.

Yield: 3 quarts

4 fresh jalapeño peppers,
   cut in thirds on the diagonal
1 garlic bulb, unpeeled, cut in half
   horizontally
4 carrots (1 1/2 pounds), peeled
   and cut into 1/8-inch rounds
   on the diagonal
1 onion (3/4 pound), peeled and
   cut into eighths
1/2 pound cauliflower flowerets

Marinade:
3 cups white wine vinegar
3 tablespoons salt
   Juice of 3 limes (3/4 cup)

Combine jalapeños, garlic, carrots, onion and cauliflower in a 3-quart glass jar or storage container.

To make marinade, mix vinegar, salt and lime juice in a small bowl; pour over vegetables. Cover with cold water. Seal jar and shake to mix. Keeps well in the refrigerator for 1 month.

Cactus Salad

Get ready to be pleasantly surprised by the appealing flavor of this uncommon blend of ingredients. A light and refreshing companion to Adios Gringos Chili (page 134) or Chili Rellenos (page 149), this is one of those memorable dishes that people continue to talk about especially when paired with Charbroiled Rattlesnake Tofu (page 140).

Yield: 1 1/2 quarts

2 cups Mexican "Ouchies" plus
   1/4 cup marinade (page 79)
1 small jicama* (1 pound)
1 cup bottled cactus strips,*
   drained and rinsed
1/2 cup vegetable oil
1/4 cup white wine vinegar
2 tablespoons chopped fresh
   cilantro
1/2 teaspoon dried oregano,
   crumbled
   Juice of 1 lime
1/2 cup orange juice
1/4 cup lemonade
1/4 cup Sprite
1/4 cup sugar
1/2 tablespoon salt

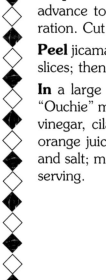

Prepare "Ouchies" at least 2 days in advance to allow for full flavor maturation. Cut into bite-size pieces.

Peel jicama and cut into 1/4-inch-thick slices; then into 1-inch triangles.

In a large bowl, combine "Ouchies," "Ouchie" marinade, jicama, cactus, oil, vinegar, cilantro, oregano, lime juice, orange juice, lemonade, Sprite, sugar and salt; marinate 2 to 3 hours before serving.

*Available in Hispanic markets.

Mixed Greens with Bleu Cheese and Roasted Walnuts

The fresh, clean taste of a leafy green salad is a good way to begin any meal.
Choose from a wide variety of greens available in most supermarkets.
Substitute the bleu cheese with feta, goat cheese, Cheddar or Swiss.
Use pine nuts, almonds, pistachios or hazelnuts in place of the walnuts.
In short, feel free to be creative with ingredients you may already have on hand.

Yield: 8 to 10 servings

1 cup dressing

Dressing:
- 1/4 cup chopped fresh Italian parsley, packed
- 2 tablespoons finely chopped scallions
- 2 teaspoons minced garlic
- 1 tablespoon Dijon mustard
- 7 tablespoons walnut oil
- 1/4 cup rice vinegar
- 1 teaspoon sugar
- 1 teaspoon salt
- Freshly ground black pepper

- 6 quarts assorted lettuce greens, washed and dried, cut or torn into bite-size pieces (romaine, bibb, arugula, red leaf, endive, raddichio)
- 3 ounces crumbled bleu cheese (about 1 cup)
- 1 cup roasted walnuts (page 12)

To make dressing, combine parsley, scallions, garlic, mustard, oil, vinegar, sugar and salt in a small bowl; adjust seasonings with pepper, as desired. Whisk to incorporate ingredients; toss with lettuce greens. Sprinkle each serving with 1 tablespoon cheese and 1 tablespoon nuts.

Mandarin Lettuce Salad

*Sweet and tart, this crisp, zesty
combination makes a lively companion to
Chilled Sesame Noodles (page 148)
or Crêpes Champignons (page 150).*

Yield: 8 servings

1/3 cup rice vinegar
1 cup vegetable oil
1/4 cup sugar
1 teaspoon salt
1 teaspoon dry mustard
1/2 tablespoon onion powder
2 teaspoons poppy seeds
6 quarts romaine, cut or torn into
   1 1/2-inch pieces (about 2 to 3
   large heads)
1 cup slivered toasted almonds
   (page 12)
2 cans (11 ounces each) mandarin
   orange sections, drained

Combine vinegar, oil, sugar, salt, mustard, onion powder and poppy seeds in a small bowl; whisk to incorporate ingredients. Toss with romaine in a large bowl.

Sprinkle individual servings with almonds and mandarin orange sections.

Cantaloupe and Tomato Salad with Avocado

Experiment with an uncommon mingling of fruit.
For maximum pleasure and goodness, capture the flavors of this salad
in the summer when ingredients are at their peak.

Yield: 3 quarts

1 to 2 cantaloupes (totaling 5½ pounds), peeled, seeded and cut into ½-inch bite-size pieces	**Combine** cantaloupe, tomatoes, avocados, scallions, cilantro and lemon vinaigrette in a large bowl. Chill 2 hours before serving.
8 roma tomatoes (2 pounds), cut into ½ inch bite-size pieces	
2 to 3 avocados (1½ pounds), peeled and cut into ½-inch chunks	
3 tablespoons thinly sliced scallions	
¼ cup chopped fresh cilantro, packed	
1 recipe Lemon Vinaigrette (3 cups) (page 88)	

Minted Waldorf Salad

Celebrate this gathering of crisp celery,
tart sweet apples and crunchy roasted nuts laced with
minted creamy dressing. Serve with a sandwich of toasted
dark rye bread, bleu cheese, cucumbers and sprouts.

Yield: 7 cups

3/4 cup mayonnaise
2 teaspoons lemon juice
1/4 cup sugar
1/2 teaspoon salt
4 tablespoons chopped fresh mint,
   or 2 teaspoons dried, crumbled
1 cup heavy cream
4 Granny Smith apples, cored and
   cut into bite-size pieces
1 cup diced celery (1/4-inch dice)
1 cup coarsely chopped walnuts
  Salt

Combine mayonnaise, lemon juice, sugar, salt and mint in a medium bowl. Whip cream using a wire whisk or electric mixer; add to mayonnaise mixture.

Stir to incorporate ingredients; add apples, celery and walnuts. Adjust seasonings with salt, as desired.

Fresh Fruit
with Strawberry Vinaigrette

Choose from a broad selection of seasonal fruit to showcase a cool and refreshing beginning or ending to any meal. Remember to allow for interesting texture and color combinations for maximum excitement.

Yield: 3 quarts fruit

2 cups vinaigrette

Vinaigrette:
- 1/2 cup fresh or frozen strawberries, thawed
- 1 cup vegetable oil
- 1/2 cup rice vinegar
- 1/2 teaspoon salt
- 1 tablespoon sugar
- 2 teaspoons minced fresh gingerroot
- 1/2 teaspoon ground fennel
- 1/8 teaspoon cayenne pepper
- 2 tablespoons orange juice

- 1 honeydew melon (3 1/4 pounds), peeled, seeded and cut into 3/4-inch bite-size pieces
- 3 pounds nectarines, pitted and cut into 3/4-inch bite-size pieces
- 4 Bartlett pears, cored and cut into 3/4-inch bite-size pieces
- 2 pints fresh strawberries, cut in half lengthwise; stems removed
- Fresh mint for garnish

In a small bowl, combine strawberries, oil, vinegar, salt, sugar, gingerroot, fennel, cayenne and orange juice in blender; purée 10 to 15 seconds.

Combine honeydew, nectarines, pears and strawberries in a large bowl. Toss with dressing.

Garnish individual servings with fresh mint.

Red Wine Vinaigrette

The use of good-quality red wine vinegar and olive oil make all the difference in this snappy vinaigrette permeated with fresh herbs. Excellent as a marinade for tofu, tempeh and assorted vegetables.

Yield: 1 1/2 cups

1 1/4 cups olive oil
  2 tablespoons plus 2 teaspoons
      lemon juice
 1/3 cup red wine vinegar
  2 tablespoons plus 2 teaspoons
      Dijon mustard
  1 teaspoon minced garlic
  3 tablespoons chopped fresh dill,
      or 1 teaspoon dried, crumbled
  3 tablespoons chopped fresh basil,
      or 1 teaspoon dried, crumbled
  3 tablespoons chopped fresh
      tarragon, or 1/2 teaspoon
      dried, crumbled
  1 tablespoon sugar
 1/2 teaspoon salt

Mix together oil, lemon juice, vinegar, mustard, garlic, dill, basil, tarragon, sugar and 1/2 teaspoon salt or to taste in a medium bowl; whisk to incorporate ingredients. Chill until ready to serve.

Fruit Vinaigrette

Choose from an elaborate array of fresh, frozen or preserved fruits including strawberries, raspberries, blackberries, blueberries, apricots, mangoes, papayas and passion fruit available in most supermarkets. Be creative when arranging the fruit; then drizzle with Fruit Vinaigrette or use it as a dressing on fresh, leafy greens.

Yield: 2 cups

1/4 cup puréed fruit
1 cup vegetable oil
1/2 cup rice vinegar
1/2 teaspoon salt
1 tablespoon sugar
1/2 teaspoon poppy seeds, ground
    fennel or celery seeds
1 teaspoon orange zest
2 tablespoons orange juice
2 teaspoons minced fresh
    gingerroot

Combine fruit, oil, vinegar, salt, sugar, poppy seeds, orange zest and juice and gingerroot in blender; purée 15 seconds. Chill until ready to use.

Lemon Vinaigrette

*Brighten pastas, grains, greens, vegetables and fruits
with this fragrant, sparkling dressing.*

Yield: 3 cups

Zest of 2 lemons (4 teaspoons) Juice of 4 large lemons (1 cup) 2 tablespoons sherry 2 tablespoons chopped fresh mint or fresh basil, packed 1/2 teaspoon cayenne pepper 11/2 cups virgin olive oil 4 tablespoons sugar 1 teaspoon salt	**In** a small bowl, combine lemon zest and juice, sherry, mint, cayenne, oil, sugar and salt; whisk to incorporate ingredients. Chill until ready to serve.

Chipotle Vinaigrette

*For a quick and delicious salad fix, open a can of corn and black beans
and saturate with this smoky, zesty sauce. Use this marinade for mushrooms,
roasted peppers and eggplant or toss with noodles or grains.
It is simply divine!*

Yield: 2³/4 cups

5 dried chipotle peppers,* stems
    removed
2 cups boiling water
1/2 cup orange juice
2 cups olive oil
1 cup lime juice
2 tablespoons minced garlic
1/2 cup minced onion
1 tablespoon ground roasted
    cumin (page 13)
1¹/2 teaspoons salt
1/2 teaspoon coarsely ground
    black pepper
1/4 cup sugar
1/4 cup finely chopped fresh
    cilantro, packed

Reconstitute chipotle peppers in boiling water for 20 minutes. Drain and discard water. Place peppers and orange juice in blender; purée. With motor running, slowly add 1 cup of the oil.

Combine remaining 1 cup oil, lime juice, garlic, onion, cumin, salt, pepper, sugar and cilantro in a small bowl. Add puréed mixture; whisk to incorporate ingredients. Chill at least 2 hours before serving.

*Available in Hispanic markets.

Wisconsin Bleu Cheese Dressing

A great variation to add to a collection, this recipe makes a terrific dip for fresh vegetables, crackers or chips. Try it as a sandwich spread or on focaccia, a type of Italian round bread seasoned with herbs.

Yield: 2 cups

1 cup mayonnaise
1 tablespoon apple juice
3 tablespoons rice vinegar
1/2 teaspoon minced garlic
2 tablespoons olive oil
1/2 teaspoon Worcestershire sauce
4 ounces Wisconsin bleu cheese
    (1 cup)

Combine mayonnaise, apple juice, vinegar, garlic, oil, Worcestershire and cheese in a food processor; process until smooth. Chill until ready to serve.

Creamy Pesto Dressing

Here's a quick and easy idea for pasta salad, potato salad, vegetables or mixed greens. Simply combine your favorite pesto with mayonnaise and lemon juice in the proportions listed below. Try this recipe with Basil Pesto (page 47), Cilantro Pesto (page 48) or Sundried Tomato Pesto (page 50) as a delicious dip for vegetables, crackers or chips.

Yield: 2 cups

1 cup pesto
1 cup mayonnaise
4 tablespoons lemon juice

In a small bowl, combine pesto, mayonnaise and lemon juice; whisk to incorporate ingredients. Chill until ready to use.

Moroccan Shish Kabobs

Sensational skewers of marinated charbroiled tofu and vegetables served with Minted Couscous (page 117) and Hummus (page 34).

(Recipe on page 142)

Crêpes Champignons

The mild, delicate flavor of crêpes filled with a richly seasoned mushroom mixture and garnished with steamed asparagus and roasted red peppers is destined to grace any table with elegance and good taste.

(Recipe on page 150)

Glorious Chocolate Cake

Vibrantly flavored and velvety smooth, the moist texture and deep richness of this confection conspire to send one into a condition of ecstatic intoxication.

(Recipe on page 166)

Poached Pears in Burgundy Wine

Steeped in the perfumed essence of spiced, hearty Burgundy, these pears can also be served with savory dishes to bring out contrasting flavors.

(Recipe on page 181)

Carrot Cake

Full of moist, fruity textures and infused with subtle, sweet spices, this homey baked treat loves its sugary coat of cream cheese frosting.

(Recipe on page 165)

Cloud 9

A celestial endeavor featuring strips of dark chocolate sponge cake buried in an avalanche of white chocolate mousse.

(Recipe on page 170)

Norimaki with Vegetables

In traditional Japanese sushi-making, the nori is prepared with raw fish. Sample this vegetarian translation using scallions, cucumbers, carrots and eggs.

(Recipe on page 28)

Seitan Smoked Virginia Ham

Reminiscent of smoked ham, the texture and flavor of this seitan recipe are ideally suited to a host of zesty condiments and salsas.

(Recipe on page 125)

Chapter 7

Companion Dishes

Vegetables, Grains and Beans

Autumn Harvest Medley

*Enjoy this quartet of roasted root vegetables as is or accented with
Mustard Sauce (page 54), Alfredo Sauce with Fresh Herbs (page 52)
or Cranberry Relish (page 44). The chewy nuttiness of wild rice or
Kasha and Brown Rice Pilaf (page 116) makes a
perfect partner for these pungent,
aromatic, cold-weather vegetables.*

Yield: 8 servings

4 parsnips, uniform in size
    (1 pound)
4 carrots, uniform in size
    (1 pound)
2 turnips, uniform in size
    (3/4 pound)
1 large rutabaga (1 1/4 pounds)
1 large onion (3/4 pound)
6 whole garlic cloves, peeled
3 tablespoons olive oil
2 teaspoons dried dill, crumbled
1 tablespoon fennel seed
2 teaspoons salt
1 teaspoon coarsely ground
    black pepper

Preheat oven to 400 degrees F.

Peel and trim ends of parsnips and carrots. Cut each in half horizontally, then vertically to obtain 16 pieces of each vegetable. Peel turnips and cut into eighths to obtain 16 pieces. Peel rutabaga and cut into quarters. Cut each quarter into fourths to obtain 16 pieces. Peel onion and slice into 1/2-inch strips.

In a large bowl, combine parsnips, carrots, turnips, rutabagas, onion, garlic cloves, oil, dill, fennel seed, salt and pepper. Using hands, rub seasonings into vegetables until well coated. Transfer vegetables to an 18x12-inch roasting pan and cover with foil. Bake 20 minutes. Remove foil and roast an additional 30 to 40 minutes or until vegetables are tender, but firm.

Tangy Acorn Squash

Choose from a broad selection of winter squash to sample the velvety texture and deep, sweet richness of this recipe. An excellent addition to a Thanksgiving feast, it is easy to prepare and has a refrigerated shelf life of one week. The flavor of the squash improves the longer it marinates.

Yield: 8 servings

2 acorn squash (approximately
    1¼ pounds each)
4 tablespoons butter
½ cup lemon juice
1 cup orange juice
2 cups water
½ cup firmly packed brown sugar
½ teaspoon ground nutmeg
¼ teaspoon ground cinnamon
⅛ teaspoon ground cloves
1½ teaspoons salt

Preheat oven to 400 degrees F.

Quarter each squash and remove seeds. Place sections in a 10x12-inch baking pan, cut side up.

In a small saucepan, combine butter, lemon juice, orange juice, water, brown sugar, nutmeg, cinnamon, cloves and salt. Bring to a boil over medium heat, stirring occasionally. Pour sauce over squash and cover with foil. Bake approximately 45 minutes or until squash is fork-tender. Remove from oven; discard foil and allow to cool. Store squash in cooking liquid; marinate 24 hours in refrigerator. Reheat in microwave or in moderate 350-degree F oven for 10 minutes or until just heated through.

Charbroiled Vegetables

Here's an outstanding signature dish. These succulent, aromatic vegetables have a Southwestern accent that exude a smoky, seared fragrance, which is enhanced by the homemade Barbecue Sauce (page 57). Serve these vegetables hot or cold in soups, with salads, pastas, grains or as appetizers. They are recommended as an accompaniment to Adios Gringos Chili (page 134), Seitan Smoked Virginia Ham (page 125), Meat Loaf (page 129), Quinoa with Fresh Cilantro (page 115), Mediterranean Rice (page 114) and on and on. The vegetables may be prepared a day or two in advance and reheated in a microwave or moderate 350-degree F oven. They keep well in the refrigerator for one week.

Yield: 8 servings

4 small zucchini (6 ounces each) or
   2 large zucchini
   (12 ounces each)
1 large eggplant (1 pound)
2 carrots (8 ounces each),
   10 to 12 inches long
2 large Granny Smith apples

Apple marinade:
4 tablespoons Barbecue Sauce
   (page 57), or commercial
   barbecue sauce
2 tablespoons olive oil
1/4 teaspoon salt

Vegetable marinade:
1 cup Barbecue Sauce (page 57),
   or commercial barbecue sauce
1/4 cup olive oil
1 tablespoon minced garlic
1 tablespoon dried oregano,
   crumbled
1 tablespoon whole fennel seeds
1 teaspoon salt
1/2 teaspoon ground black pepper

Cut small zucchini in half lengthwise or for larger zucchini, cut on the diagonal into 8 long slices, 3/4 inch thick. Trim stem and bottom off eggplant and discard. Slice in half lengthwise and then into 3/4-inch-thick half-moons (14 to 16 pieces). Peel carrots and cut on the diagonal to obtain 10 slices each (5 inches long and 1/4 inch thick). Slice apples into 8 even rings and remove cores.

To prepare apple marinade, mix Barbecue Sauce, oil and salt in a small bowl. Add apple rings and coat thoroughly.

To prepare vegetable marinade, mix Barbecue Sauce, oil, garlic, oregano, fennel seeds, salt and pepper in a large bowl. Add vegetables; stir until well mixed.

Grill vegetables and apples over hot coals or arrange on a cookie sheet and bake in a 400-degree F oven for 15 minutes. Zucchini, carrots and apples should be crisp-tender. The eggplant will take several minutes longer and should be tender, but not overcooked to the point of collapsing.

Braised Leeks

*In this recipe, the mild, subtle-flavored member of the onion family
makes its appearance as a side dish, but easily doubles as a chilled appetizer.
Leeks should be stored in their own cooking liquid to improve flavor.
For variation, substitute butter for the olive oil; tarragon, dill or fennel
for the thyme; and lemon juice for the vinegar. Remember, butter congeals
when cold, so if serving this dish chilled, use olive oil. Cooked leeks keep
well in the refrigerator for three to four days.*

Yield: 8 servings

4 large leeks or 8 small ones
 (12 inches long)
1 tablespoon vegetarian chicken-
 flavored powder
1 cup boiling water
4 whole garlic cloves, peeled and
 thinly sliced
2 bay leaves
1/4 cup olive oil
3 tablespoons Spanish sherry
 vinegar or good-quality
 red wine vinegar
2 teaspoons dried thyme, crumbled
1/2 teaspoon salt
1/2 teaspoon coarsely ground
 black pepper
 Olive oil for browning

Preheat oven to 400 degrees F.

Trim roots from leeks; cut close to the white portion. (Do not cut through white. This will keep leeks intact when slicing lengthwise.) Make diagonal cuts through green tops of leek, leaving an 8- to 10-inch overall length. Split leek in half lengthwise. Wash well to remove any sand or grit and place in a shallow roasting pan.

Prepare broth by dissolving vegetarian chicken-flavored powder and boiling water in a small bowl; add garlic, bay leaves, oil, vinegar, thyme, salt and pepper. Stir well and pour over leeks. Bake 55 to 60 minutes or until leeks are tender, but firm.

To serve, coat bottom of a large skillet or griddle with oil; brown leeks and fold into a v-shape. Garnish with a slice of Roasted Red and Yellow Peppers (page 16).

Honeyed Apples Stuffed with Red Cabbage

Enjoy the tart sweetness of a baked Granny Smith apple
filled with tangy braised cabbage and a hint of caraway.
This colorful dish is pleasing to look at as well as tasty to eat.
An essential accompaniment to Mushroom Potato Stroganoff (page 162),
this side dish is also perfect with Tofu Chicken Paprikash (page 138).

Yield: 8 stuffed apples

8 large Granny Smith apples

Marinade:
   1 cup apple juice
   1/2 cup red wine
   1/2 cup honey
   1 teaspoon salt

Filling:
   1 medium red cabbage (3 pounds)
   1 large Granny Smith apple
   3 tablespoons vegetable oil
   1/2 cup finely chopped onion
   2 tablespoons vegetarian chicken-
      flavored powder
   1/2 cup boiling water
   1/3 cup red wine vinegar
   1 bay leaf
   1/2 tablespoon caraway seeds
   1/2 tablespoon salt
   2 tablespoons white wine
   1 tablespoon lemon juice
   1/3 cup brown sugar
   2 tablespoons honey
   1 teaspoon ground black pepper
   1 teaspoon salt

Preheat oven to 400 degrees F.

To prepare apples, cut top third off each apple and reserve for filling. Using a melon baller, scoop out core and apple flesh, leaving approximately 1/2 inch of flesh around perimeter.

To make marinade, in a small bowl, combine apple juice, red wine, honey and salt. Place apples in a baking pan and pour 1/4 cup marinade into each apple. Bake uncovered 20 minutes. Remove from oven and baste apples with cooked marinade. Return pan to oven; continue baking 10 minutes more or until apples are tender, but firm and retain their shape. (Overcooking will cause apples to collapse and lose their shape.) Remove apples from oven; set aside.

To make filling, remove outer wilted leaves of cabbage and discard. Cut cabbage into quarters, remove core and thinly slice. Peel reserved apple tops and whole apple. Remove core and thinly slice.

Heat oil in a 5-quart saucepan; add onion and sauté until translucent. Prepare broth by dissolving vegetarian chicken-flavored powder in boiling water; stir into saucepan and add cabbage and sliced apples. Cover and cook over high heat 2 to 3 minutes until cabbage begins to wilt. Add vinegar, bay leaf, caraway seeds, salt, white wine, lemon juice, brown sugar and honey; bring to a boil. Reduce heat and simmer 20 to 30 minutes until cabbage is tender, but still crunchy. Adjust seasonings with pepper and 1 teaspoon salt or to taste. Remove from heat and stuff apples generously with filling. Serve warm.

Mexican Corn Cobbets

This unique creation was the result of our cook's passion for a tender, sweet ear of corn on the cob. Serve as a garnish on Charbroiled Rattlesnake Tofu (page 140) or Chili Rellenos (page 149) or include as part of a mixed vegetable platter of Charbroiled Vegetables (page 102), Braised Leeks (page 103), Tangy Acorn Squash (page 101), Indonesian Cabbage (page 108) and Grilled Garlic Mushrooms (page 109).

Yield: 24 pieces

Sauce:
   1 cup mayonnaise
   Juice of 1 lime (1/4 cup)
   Zest of 1 lemon (2 teaspoons)
   1 tablespoon Western Spice
     (page 57)
1 1/2 teaspoons salt

   8 ears corn
   2 tablespoons sugar
 3/4 cup grated Parmesan cheese
   1 lime, cut in eighths

Mix mayonnaise, lime juice, lemon zest, Western Spice and salt in a small bowl.

Cut each ear of corn into thirds and place in a kettle of boiling water (to cover) with the sugar. Cook 5 minutes over high heat. Drain and grill corn over hot coals or under a broiler until lightly charred.

Roll corn in the sauce and then in Parmesan. Serve with lime wedge to squeeze over corn.

Polenta Stuffed Chayote

*Chayote squash, native to Mexico and Central America,
is a delicate, light green, pear-shaped, fleshy fruit with a single flat seed.
In this recipe, seasoned polenta, a type of cornmeal pudding popular in
Northern Italy, is used as a filling. This side dish may be served as is
or topped with Alfredo Sauce with Fresh Herbs (page 52), Hot Orange Sauce
(page 55) or Tulsa Salsa (page 39). The chayote is delicious simply
steamed with a little butter. The polenta is good on its own
or as a companion to Braised Leeks (page 103)
and Charbroiled Vegetables (page 102).*

Yield: 8 servings

4 large chayote squash*

Polenta filling:
2 tablespoons butter
1/4 cup thinly sliced scallions
1/4 cup diced red pepper
1/2 teaspoon fennel seeds
1/2 tablespoon vegetarian chicken-
flavored powder
3 cups boiling water
1/2 teaspoon dried dill, crumbled
1 cup yellow cornmeal
1/2 cup shredded Monterey Jack
cheese
1/2 cup frozen corn kernels, thawed
Salt and pepper

Steam chayotes until fork-tender (30 minutes) in a small amount of water using a saucepan with a tight-fitting lid. Drain and cool. Slice chayote in half lengthwise. Using a melon baller, scoop out seeds and some of the flesh, leaving a 1/2-inch border around the perimeter.

Heat butter in a heavy-bottomed 4-quart saucepan. Add scallions, red pepper, and fennel seeds; sauté over medium heat 1 minute. Prepare vegetarian broth by dissolving vegetarian chicken-flavored powder in boiling water; stir into saucepan. Add dill and bring to a boil. Slowly drizzle in cornmeal, whisking continuously to prevent lumps from forming. Reduce heat; add Jack cheese and cook an additional 2 minutes, stirring frequently. Add corn and adjust seasonings with salt and pepper. Remove from heat and spoon polenta filling into chayote.

*Available in specialty produce section of supermarkets or Asian and Hispanic markets.

Eggplant With Cilantro and Roasted Cumin

This basic recipe was passed on to one of our cooks by a Moroccan friend and has been slightly revised to allow for easy preparation. Lovers of eggplant, cilantro and cumin rejoice! This is an exotic, passionate composition, permeated with deep, pungent aromas. Very Casablanca-esque. Serve hot with Minted Couscous (page 117) or cold, tossed with kalamata olives, feta or chèvre.

Yield: 8 servings

1 cup Cilantro Cumin Sauce

Cilantro Cumin Sauce:
- 1 tablespoon plus 1 teaspoon ground roasted cumin (page 13)
- 2 cups fresh cilantro leaves, washed and lightly packed
- 1 teaspoon minced garlic
- 1/2 cup virgin olive oil
- 3 tablespoons fresh lemon juice
- 2 teaspoons salt

- 2 eggplant (1 pound each)
- 3 teaspoons salt
- 1 large onion (1 pound)
- 2 red peppers (1 pound)
- 2 yellow peppers (1 pound)
- 1 tablespoon minced garlic
- 1/3 cup virgin olive oil
- 2 teaspoons freshly ground black pepper

To make sauce, combine cumin, cilantro, garlic, oil, lemon juice and salt in food processor; process until smooth.

Cut stems and bottoms off eggplant and discard. Slice in half lengthwise and then into 3/4-inch-thick half-moons. Place slices on a rack over a shallow pan. Salt both sides lightly with 2 teaspoons of the salt and allow to drain for 1 hour. Peel and slice onion into 1-inch strips. Seed and slice peppers into 1-inch strips. Rinse eggplant slices and pat dry.

Preheat oven to 400 degrees F.

Combine eggplant, onion, peppers, remaining 1 teaspoon salt, garlic, oil and black pepper in a large bowl; toss until well coated.

Place seasoned vegetables on a cookie sheet and bake uncovered for 30 minutes or until eggplant is tender, not mushy. Cool and toss with Cilantro Cumin Sauce; marinate overnight in refrigerator. Grill vegetables on a griddle until warmed through. Reheat in a moderate 350-degree F oven or in a skillet using a little olive oil. Serve warm or at room temperature.

Indonesian Cabbage

*Delight family or friends by offering an unexpected cabbage concoction.
Heady with the scent of fresh gingerroot, garlic and coconut cream,
this recipe is guaranteed to convert the staunch cabbage-hater into a lively
supporter of the leafy garden plant. Serve warm with white rice, lentils, Quinoa
with Fresh Cilantro (page 115), Kasha and Brown Rice Pilaf (page 116) or
serve cold, tossed with noodles and seasoned tofu. Easy and quick to prepare,
it keeps well in the refrigerator for one week.*

Yield: 10 cups

1 medium green cabbage (3 pounds)
2 tablespoons vegetable oil
1 large onion (1 pound),
   peeled and sliced
2 teaspoons minced garlic
2 teaspoons minced fresh
   gingerroot
1 1/2 teaspoons turmeric
1 teaspoon vegetarian chicken-
   flavored powder
1/2 cup boiling water
1/4 cup coconut cream*
2 teaspoons salt
1/2 teaspoon ground white pepper
1 cup shredded sweetened coconut

Cut cabbage into quarters, remove core and discard. Slice into 1/2-inch strips.

Heat oil in an 8-quart saucepan and sauté onion until wilted. Add garlic, gingerroot and turmeric; cook 30 seconds. Prepare broth by dissolving vegetarian chicken-flavored powder in boiling water; stir into saucepan. Add coconut cream, cabbage and salt; mix to combine ingredients. Cover and cook over medium heat 8 to 10 minutes or until cabbage is crisp-tender. Adjust seasonings with salt and pepper, as desired.

Preheat oven to 350 degrees F.

Place coconut on a cookie sheet and toast in oven for several minutes or until golden brown; cool.

Sprinkle individual servings with 1 to 2 tablespoons toasted coconut.

*Available in liquor stores or
liquor department of supermarkets.
For best results, we prefer
La Preferida coconut cream.

Grilled Garlic Mushrooms

Nothing is easier to prepare than this recipe. Fresh minced garlic has a tendency to burn under the broiler and is not recommended. This simple trio of fresh mushrooms, anointed with olive oil and garlic, is heaven scent. Savor with a baked potato and tossed salad for a quick, light repast.

Yield: 8 cups mushrooms

2 pounds mushrooms* (uniform in size), stems removed and discarded
1/2 cup olive oil
2 tablespoons garlic powder
1/2 teaspoon salt
Freshly ground black pepper

Wipe mushrooms clean with a damp paper towel. (If shiitake mushrooms are large, slice in half.) Quarter or slice Portobello mushrooms into 1/2- to 3/4-inch-thick slices.

Combine oil and garlic powder in a large bowl; toss with mushrooms. Place mushrooms in a shallow baking pan and broil 5 to 6 minutes until done or grill on a hot griddle.

Sprinkle with 1/2 teaspoon salt or to taste and pepper, as desired; serve immediately.

Note: Choose fresh button, shiitake or Portobello mushrooms or a combination of mushrooms.

Wild Rice with Portobello Mushrooms

The diverse flavors and textures of this hearty grain dish emerge in bold, full-bodied goodness. A gathering of elements that is basic, simple and elegant all in one. This recipe performs well with Tangy Acorn Squash (page 101), Autumn Harvest Medley (page 100) and Braised Leeks (page 103).

Yield: 10 servings

2 tablespoons plus 2 teaspoons vegetarian chicken-flavored powder
5 cups boiling water
2 cups wild rice
1 bay leaf
4 ounces sundried tomatoes (1 cup sliced)
1 cup Uncle Ben's Converted White Rice
1/2 pound Portobello mushrooms (5 mushrooms, approximately 2 1/2 inches in diameter)
1/2 pound carrots
2 tablespoons butter
2 tablespoons olive oil
1 1/2 cups chopped onion
1 tablespoon minced garlic
1/4 teaspoon salt
1/2 teaspoon coarsely ground black pepper

In a heavy-bottomed 4-quart saucepan, prepare broth by dissolving vegetarian chicken-flavored powder in boiling water; add 3 1/2 cups of the vegetarian broth, wild rice and bay leaf. Cover and bring to a boil. Reduce heat and simmer approximately 45 minutes or until rice is tender, but chewy.

Using a scissors, snip tomatoes into 1/8-inch-wide strips lengthwise; add to cooked rice and stir. Discard bay leaf; cover pan and set aside.

In a small covered saucepan, combine white rice and remaining 1 1/2 cups vegetarian broth; bring to a boil. Reduce heat and simmer approximately 25 minutes or until liquid has been absorbed and rice is tender, but chewy (at The Cheese Factory, rice is served al dente).

Remove stems from Portobellos and discard. Cut mushrooms into 1/4-inch slices. Peel and julienne carrots.

Heat butter and oil in a 10-inch skillet. Add onion and garlic; sauté 1 to 2 minutes over medium-high heat. Add Portobellos; sauté 2 to 3 minutes. Add carrots; sprinkle with salt and sauté 1 minute more. Add white and wild rice to skillet; stir to combine. Add pepper; adjust seasonings with additional salt, as desired.

Gnocchi di Patate

(Potato Dumplings)

Bathed in Marinara Sauce (page 58), Alfredo Sauce with Fresh Herbs (page 52)
or tossed with Basil Pesto (page 47) or Sundried Tomato Pesto (pages 50),
these little nuggets of Italian ancestry offer the palate an abundance of
comforting satisfaction. Add them to soups and stews or toss with
Grilled Garlic Mushrooms (page 109). Prepare a day or two in advance,
wrap tightly and store in the refrigerator. Reheat in a microwave
or sauté in a little butter or olive oil.

Yield: 276 gnocchis

4¹/2 pounds red-skinned potatoes
¹/8 teaspoon cinnamon
5¹/2 cups flour (1³/4 pounds)
5 quarts water
2 tablespoons salt

Boil potatoes in a 5-quart saucepan until tender. Remove skins and discard. Grate potatoes using a hand grater or put through a ricer while still hot.

In a large bowl, combine grated potatoes, cinnamon and flour; mix well by hand. (The mixture will be quite sticky.) Dust work surface with additional flour to prevent dough from sticking. Shape dough into 23 rolls (12 inches long by ³/4 inches in diameter). Cut each roll into 1-inch pieces (12 pieces per roll); mark and shape each piece, pressing lightly with the prongs of a fork. Place pieces on floured work surface (do not allow to touch or they will stick together).

Bring water to a boil in a 5-quart saucepan; add salt. Place ¹/4 of gnocchi pieces in boiling water; cook 30 seconds after they float to surface. Remove cooked gnocchi with a slotted spoon and repeat process until all gnocchis have been cooked. Cool before wrapping and refrigerating. Serve immediately or refrigerate for later use.

Cheese Factory Corn Bread

*Rich tasting, coarse textured and scented with a hint of vanilla,
this corn bread is served at the restaurant with Adios Gringos Chili (page 134).
Try it as an appetizing snack with a number of assorted spreads or sauces
including Fresh Herb Cheese Spread (page 46), Hot Orange Sauce (page 55),
Cranberry Relish (page 44) or No Known Survivors (page 56).
It freezes perfectly and reheats well in a microwave.*

Yield: 1 loaf

1 cup flour
1 cup yellow cornmeal
1 tablespoon baking powder
1 teaspoon salt
1/2 cup sugar
3 large eggs, beaten
1/2 cup buttermilk
1/2 cup milk
1/4 cup butter, melted
1 teaspoon vanilla extract

Preheat oven to 425 degrees F.

Spray a 9-inch round cake pan with nonstick cooking spray and lightly flour.

Mix flour, cornmeal, baking powder, salt and sugar in a medium bowl. In a separate bowl, combine eggs, buttermilk, milk, butter and vanilla; stir well. Add egg mixture to dry ingredients; stir just until ingredients are moistened. (Do not overmix.) Pour batter into prepared pan and bake 20 to 25 minutes until golden in color. Remove from oven and invert onto round plate. Carefully remove from plate and cool on wire rack.

Savory Corn Bread Dressing

Festive and uplifting, this recipe inspires sumptuous celebration all year-round. Imagine aromatic vegetables, fresh herbs, crisp apples and plump raisins, surrounded by chunks of homemade corn bread drenched in Country Gravy (page 53)—that's a mouthful! For a heartier version, add a cup or two of Italian Crumble Sausage (page 133) and serve with generous portions of Cranberry Relish (page 44). The dressing can be prepared two to three days in advance and reheated in a microwave or moderate 350-degree F oven.

Yield: 8 servings

1 teaspoon vegetarian chicken-flavored powder
1/2 cup boiling water
1/2 cup raisins
2 tablespoons butter
1 cup diced onion
2 teaspoons minced garlic
1 cup diced celery
1 Granny Smith apple, peeled, cored and diced
1 1/2 teaspoons salt
1 recipe Cheese Factory Corn Bread (page 112)
1/2 cup roasted walnuts or pecans (page 12), chopped
3 large eggs, beaten
4 tablespoons butter, melted
1/4 cup chopped fresh marjoram, packed or 2 teaspoons dried, crumbled
1/4 cup chopped fresh sage, packed or 2 teaspoons dried, crumbled
1 cup chopped fresh Italian parsley, packed

Preheat oven to 400 degrees F.

In a small bowl, prepare broth by dissolving vegetarian chicken-flavored powder in boiling water; add raisins and soak 20 minutes; set aside.

Heat butter in a 12-inch skillet; add onion, garlic, celery, apples and 1/2 teaspoon of the salt. Sauté 2 to 3 minutes over medium-high heat. (If using dried herbs, add now.) Sauté 30 seconds; remove skillet from heat.

Crumble corn bread into a large bowl, leaving some chunks larger than others.

Stir vegetarian broth and raisins, nuts, eggs, butter, remaining 1 teaspoon salt and fresh herbs into mixing bowl with corn bread. Pour skillet ingredients over corn bread and mix well to combine. Spray a 10x12-inch baking dish with nonstick cooking spray; place dressing in dish and bake uncovered 30 to 45 minutes.

Note: Curly parsley may be used if Italian is unavailable, but do not use dried.

Cheese Factory Corn Bread may be prepared ahead and frozen; thaw before using.

Mediterranean Rice

*The fresh Italian parsley and lemon zest are
key ingredients in this recipe. Curly parsley may be used,
but it will not be as aromatic. This savory side dish sparkles
as a stuffing for eggplant or grape leaves. It may be prepared
one or two days in advance and reheated in a microwave.
(Reheating in the oven tends to dry out
the rice and is not recommended.)*

Yield: 10 servings

3 tablespoons olive oil
2 cups finely chopped onion
2 teaspoons dried dill, crumbled
1 teaspoon dried basil, crumbled
1 teaspoon dried thyme, crumbled
2 tablespoons vegetarian chicken-
    flavored powder
4 1/2 cups boiling water
3 cups Uncle Ben's Converted
    White Rice
2 bay leaves
    Zest of 1 lemon (2 teaspoons)
1 teaspoon coarsely ground
    black pepper
2 teaspoons salt
3 tablespoons coarsely chopped
    fresh Italian parsley

Heat oil in a 5-quart saucepan; add onion and sauté 1 minute or until onion turns translucent. Add dill, basil and thyme; cook 1 minute more over medium-high heat.

In a small bowl, prepare broth by dissolving vegetarian chicken-flavored powder in boiling water; stir into saucepan. Add rice and bay leaves; cover pan and bring to a boil. Reduce heat and simmer approximately 20 minutes or until all liquid has been absorbed, and rice is tender, but chewy. Add lemon zest, pepper, 2 teaspoons salt or to taste and parsley; mix well.

Quinoa with Fresh Cilantro

*Cultivated in the Andes for centuries, quinoa has been called the
"ancient food of the Incas." Highly nutritious, this grain looks like
couscous and has a distinctive earthy, nutty flavor. It is easy to prepare
and makes a great chilled grain salad. This recipe may be prepared
one or two days ahead of time and reheated in a microwave.
It keeps well in the refrigerator for five days.*

Yield: 8 cups

1 pound quinoa (2 1/2 cups)
1 tablespoon olive oil
1 tablespoon butter
1 cup finely chopped onion
2 tablespoons vegetarian chicken-
   flavored powder
3 1/2 cups boiling water
1 bay leaf
1/2 cup chopped fresh cilantro,
   firmly packed
1/2 teaspoon ground white pepper
   Salt

Place quinoa in a sieve and rinse under cold running water; drain and set aside.

Heat oil and butter in a 4-quart saucepan; add onion. Sauté until onion turns translucent.

In a small bowl, prepare broth by dissolving vegetarian chicken-flavored powder in boiling water; stir into saucepan. Add quinoa and bay leaf. Cover pan and bring to a boil. Reduce heat and simmer approximately 20 to 30 minutes or until quinoa is tender and fluffy; remove from heat. Add cilantro and pepper. Adjust with additional salt, as desired.

Kasha and Brown Rice Pilaf

Kasha (buckwheat groats) is a soft-textured grain with a
mild and nutty flavor which is intensified by oven-toasting.
Prominent in Eastern Europe and the Soviet Union, kasha harmonizes
well with the firm, chewy character of brown rice. This blend of plump grains,
raisins and roasted nuts is delicious at room temperature or hot off the stove.
Enjoy this recipe as a side dish or use as a stuffing.
It keeps well in the refrigerator for one week.

Yield: 12 servings

1 cup raisins
1 1/2 cups (12 ounces) long grain
     brown rice
3 cups water
1/2 teaspoon salt
2 cups (1 pound) kasha*
1 large egg, slightly beaten
2 tablespoons vegetarian chicken-
     flavored powder
4 cups boiling water

Dressing:
2 tablespoons roasted tahini*
     (sesame butter)
1 tablespoon dark sesame oil
1 tablespoon lemon juice
1 tablespoon soy sauce or tamari
2 tablespoons vegetable oil
1 cup toasted walnuts (page 12)
1 cup thinly sliced scallions

Soak raisins in 2 cups hot water for 20 minutes. Drain and set aside.

To make rice, combine rice, water and salt in a heavy-bottomed 4-quart saucepan with tight-fitting lid. Bring to a boil over high heat. Reduce heat and simmer 45 minutes until water has been absorbed and rice is tender.

Preheat oven to 400 degrees F.

To prepare kasha, place in a shallow baking pan and toast in oven until golden brown and fragrant, about 5 to 10 minutes. Transfer toasted kasha to a medium saucepan; add egg. Mix until kasha groats are well coated. (This process prevents kasha groats from sticking together.)

In a small bowl, prepare broth by dissolving vegetarian chicken-flavored powder in boiling water; stir into saucepan. Cover and bring to a boil. Reduce heat and simmer 15 minutes or until liquid has been absorbed and kasha is tender.

To make dressing, in a small bowl, combine tahini, sesame oil, lemon juice, soy sauce and vegetable oil; whisk to incorporate ingredients.

Combine raisins, rice, kasha, dressing, nuts and scallions in a large bowl; toss until well blended. Serve immediately or refrigerate for later use. Reheat in microwave or a moderate 350-degree F oven.

*Available in natural food markets.

Minted Couscous

African in origin, couscous is a type of hard wheat semolina
which may be employed in the same way as rice.
It easily absorbs a wide range of distinctive flavors and is
a favorite complement to Moroccan Shish Kabobs (page 142)
or Eggplant with Cilantro and Roasted Cumin (page 107).
It can be prepared one to two days ahead
and reheated in a microwave.

Yield: 8 servings

3¹/2 cups water
1¹/2 tablespoons dried thyme,
    crumbled
¹/2 cup olive oil
¹/2 teaspoon salt
2¹/2 cups couscous
¹/4 cup chopped fresh mint, packed,
    or 2 teaspoons dried, crumbled
Freshly ground black pepper

Bring water to a boil in a 5-quart saucepan; add thyme, oil and ¹/2 teaspoon salt or to taste. Remove from heat; add couscous. Cover pan; let stand 10 minutes or until couscous has absorbed all liquid and is tender and fluffy. Add mint; adjust seasonings with pepper, as desired.

Dal

(Lentils Laced with Aromatic Vegetables and Spices)

*Legumes can be grouped into three categories: lentils, beans and peas,
all of which are called dal in Hindi. The lentil, native to Asia Minor,
has been cultivated in India since ancient times. It has an average
protein content of 22 percent by weight and thus comprises the staple
of vegetarian diets. This simple recipe may be served with fluffy plain
white rice and a vegetable side dish, such as Autumn Harvest Medley
(page 100), Tangy Acorn Squash (page 101), Indonesian Cabbage (page 108)
or Chilled Sesame Spinach (page 76). The Dal keeps well
in the refrigerator for one week.*

Yield: 10 servings

1 tablespoon vegetable oil
1 tablespoon butter
1 1/2 cups finely chopped onion
2 teaspoons minced garlic
1 1/2 tablespoons minced fresh
    gingerroot
1 cup diced carrot (1/4-inch dice)
1 cup diced celery (1/4-inch dice)
1 tablespoon roasted ground
    coriander seeds* (page 13)
1/2 teaspoon turmeric
1 teaspoon curry powder
3 tablespoons vegetarian chicken-
    flavored powder
2 quarts boiling water
2 cups lentils
1 large potato (12 ounces), peeled
    and diced 1/4-inch (2 cups)
1/4 teaspoon ground cinnamon
2 teaspoons whole roasted cumin
    seeds (page 13)
Salt and pepper
	Heat oil and butter in a heavy-bottomed 4-quart saucepan. Add onion, garlic, gingerroot, carrot and celery; sauté over high heat until onion turns translucent. Add coriander, turmeric and curry powder; cook 30 seconds.
	
	Prepare broth by dissolving vegetarian chicken-flavored powder in boiling water; stir into saucepan. Add lentils and potatoes; cover pan and bring to a boil. Reduce heat and simmer 25 to 30 minutes until lentils are tender. Add cinnamon and cumin seeds; adjust seasonings with salt and pepper, as desired.

*Available in Asian markets.

Spicy Black Beans

*A symphony of smoky, savory sensations, these black beans
are destined to be featured in burritos, enchiladas or tacos. Perfect with
Chili Rellenos (page 149), Charbroiled Rattlesnake Tofu (page 140)
or simply with a bowl of steamed white rice and a vegetable companion.
This recipe can be prepared in advance, keeps well in the refrigerator
for five days and freezes perfectly.*

Yield: 8 servings

3 dried chipotle peppers,*
   stems removed
1 cup orange juice
3 tablespoons vegetable oil
1 cup finely chopped onion
1 tablespoon minced garlic
1 cup diced carrot
1 cup diced celery
1 cup diced green pepper
1 teaspoon roasted ground cumin
   (page 13)
1 teaspoon roasted ground
   coriander (page 13)
1 teaspoon dried oregano,
   crumbled
1 teaspoon dried thyme, crumbled
16 ounces (2 cups) canned plum
   tomatoes, drained and coarsely
   chopped
56 ounces (7 cups) canned black
   beans, drained and rinsed
   Salt and pepper
1 cup chopped fresh cilantro,
   tightly packed

Reconstitute chipotle peppers in orange juice for 20 minutes. Drain; reserve orange juice and chop peppers.

Heat oil in a heavy-bottomed 5-quart saucepan. Add onion, garlic, carrot, celery and green pepper; sauté 3 to 4 minutes. Add cumin, coriander, oregano, thyme and chipotle peppers; sauté 2 to 3 minutes. Add reserved orange juice, tomatoes and black beans. Cook 10 to 15 minutes over medium heat, stirring occasionally. Adjust seasonings with salt and pepper, as desired; add fresh cilantro. Remove 1 cup bean mixture; purée in food processor until smooth and return to pan.

*Available in Hispanic markets.

Revíthia Yahní
(Chick Pea Stew with Spinach and Tomatoes)

*This recipe is an adaptation of a traditional Greek dish
that can be prepared with a minimum of fuss and enjoyed with a
maximum of enthusiasm. Chick peas, also known as garbanzos,
are a mainstay of rural life in Greece. Rich in protein and easily stored,
they sustain the villagers through the winter months and are the main
ingredients in Lenten food. Wholesome and nourishing, this dish
is great with a side of steamed white rice, Mediterranean Rice
(page 114) or Quinoa with Fresh Cilantro (page 115).
It keeps well in the refrigerator for five days.*

Yield: 8 servings

1/4 cup olive oil
1 cup onion, cut into 1-inch squares
  with layers separated
1 tablespoon minced garlic
1 tablespoon dried oregano,
  crumbled
32 ounces (4 cups) canned
  chick peas, drained and rinsed
16 ounces (2 cups) canned crushed
  Italian plum tomatoes with juice
1 bag (10 ounces) fresh spinach,
  washed and stemmed
2 teaspoons salt
1/2 teaspoon pepper
1 cup chopped fresh Italian parsley

Heat oil in a 5-quart saucepan; add onions and garlic. Sauté over medium-high heat until onion turns translucent. Add oregano, peas and tomatoes; cook 3 minutes. Stir in spinach; sauté until spinach just starts to wilt. Remove from heat; add salt, pepper and parsley. Stir until well blended.

Chapter 8

Entrées

Seitan Loaf

*Seitan is a grain-based protein alternative made from wheat gluten
(page 6). This recipe yields a chewy loaf that can be sliced and marinated for a
variety of "meaty" products. It can be prepared in large batches and frozen for
later use. Included on the following pages in this chapter are some
of the "meaty" ideas used at the restaurant.*

Yield: 1 two-pound loaf, 25 to 30 slices (1/4 inch thick)

Seitan dough:
    1 box (12 ounces) seitan mix*
    1 1/2 cups water

Seitan broth:
    1 tablespoon vegetable oil
    1 pound carrots, peeled and
        coarsely chopped
    1 large onion, peeled and coarsely
        chopped
    4 quarts water
    1 cup soy sauce or tamari
    2 teaspoons powdered ginger

To make dough, combine seitan mix and water in large bowl of electric mixer with dough hook attachment. Blend and knead mixture on low speed for about 5 minutes. (If electric mixer is unavailable, knead by hand.) Remove dough and place on work surface. Using a wooden rolling pin, beat dough vigorously for about 2 minutes. (This procedure removes excess air from dough resulting in a denser, chewier product, which resembles the desired meaty texture.) Place dough between 2 sheets of plastic wrap; roll with rolling pin into a 7- to 8-inch round shape. Remove plastic wrap. Use hands to mold or press dough into desired shape (approximately 2 1/2 to 3 inches in diameter and 8 inches long). Set aside to rest 10 minutes. (Do not roll dough—this creates air pockets, which result in a porous, spongy texture.)

To prepare broth, heat oil in an 8-quart saucepan; cook carrots and onions until brown. Add water, soy sauce and powdered ginger. Bring to a boil and immerse seitan log. Reduce heat; cover and simmer 4 hours. (Log must be covered with liquid during cooking; add additional water, if necessary.) When seitan is done (log should be firm), drain and discard broth. Chill seitan overnight in an airtight container. Seitan may also be divided into sections and frozen for later use.

Note: Slice seitan loaf diagonally to obtain longer, larger slices.

*Available in natural food markets.

Festive Seitan Turkey

Allow something special to occur at your next Thanksgiving celebration by serving a tantalizing innovation. Transform seitan into turkey and serve with Country Gravy (page 53) and Cranberry Relish (page 44). Invent fresh ideas or renew old ones by browsing through favorite turkey recipes and converting them to feature seitan as an alternative. A few good examples are turkey salad, turkey noodle soup, turkey casserole and turkey sandwiches. Get the picture?

Yield: 25 to 30 slices (1/4 inch thick)

3/4 cup vegetarian chicken-flavored
    powder
3 cups boiling water
1 tablespoon pickling spices
1 teaspoon dried rosemary,
    crumbled
1 teaspoon dried thyme, crumbled
1/2 teaspoon dried sage, crumbled
1/2 teaspoon dried marjoram,
    crumbled
1/2 teaspoon coarsely ground
    black pepper
2 whole garlic cloves,
    peeled and thinly sliced
1/4 cup vegetable oil
1 recipe seitan (page 122), or
    2 pounds commercial seitan
Vegetable or olive oil for browning

In a medium bowl, prepare broth by dissolving vegetarian chicken-flavored powder in boiling water. Add pickling spices, rosemary, thyme, sage, marjoram, pepper, garlic and oil. Cut seitan on the diagonal into 25 to 30 slices. Add seitan slices and marinate 6 to 8 hours. Drain seitan; reserve and freeze marinade for later use. Brown marinated seitan slices on griddle or in large skillet over high heat, using vegetable or olive oil mixed with a little butter.

Seitan Philly Beef

Capture an appreciative audience with a hearty mouthwatering adaptation of this popular sandwich. Excellent over rice or with mashed potatoes, this recipe hits the spot when sliced into strips and served at room temperature tossed with crisp, leafy greens or marinated vegetables. For a Mexican variation, alter marinade seasonings by substituting roasted cumin (page 13), chili powder and fresh cilantro for the basil, dill and Italian herbs. The result will be fabulous fajitas—serve with flour tortillas, Guacamole Grande (page 36) and salsa.

Yield: 8 servings

Marinade:
- 1/4 cup vegetarian beef-flavored powder
- 1 cup boiling water
- 1/2 cup olive oil
- 1/2 cup honey
- 1/2 cup A.1. steak sauce
- 1/4 cup Worcestershire sauce
- 2 tablespoons red wine vinegar
- 1 teaspoon Dijon mustard
- 2 teaspoons onion powder
- 2 teaspoons dried basil, crumbled
- 2 teaspoons dried dill, crumbled
- 2 teaspoons Italian herbs, crumbled
- 1 tablespoon salt
- 2 tablespoons finely minced garlic

- 1 recipe seitan (page 122), or 2 pounds commercial seitan

Vegetables:
- 6 tablespoons olive oil
- 1 large onion (1 pound), peeled and thinly sliced
- 2 large green peppers (1 pound), seeded, cut into 1/4-inch strips
- 2 large red peppers (1 pound), seeded, cut into 1/4-inch strips
- 1 pound sliced mushrooms

In a medium bowl, prepare broth by dissolving vegetarian beef-flavored powder in boiling water. Add oil, honey, steak sauce, Worcestershire, vinegar, mustard, onion powder, basil, dill, Italian herbs, salt and garlic. Cut seitan on the diagonal into 25 to 30 slices; add to bowl and marinate in refrigerator overnight. Drain; set aside.

To cook vegetables, heat 3 tablespoons of the oil in a 12-inch skillet; add onions and sauté 1 minute. Add peppers and mushrooms; cook over medium-high heat until vegetables are crisp-tender. Transfer to a large bowl and keep warm.

Add remaining 3 tablespoons oil to skillet; brown seitan in batches, adding additional oil as required. Combine vegetables with seitan in skillet and reheat. Serve over lightly toasted French bread.

Variation: Omit vegetarian beef-flavored powder and water; replace with 1/4 cup soy sauce mixed with 3/4 cup water.

Seitan Smoked Virginia Ham

*Reminiscent of smoked ham, the texture and flavor of this seitan recipe
is ideal with tangy fruit accompaniments, such as Broiled Fresh Pineapple
(page 180), Poached Pears in Burgundy Wine (page 181) or Cranberry Relish
(page 44). Spoon a little mustard marinade over seitan and serve hot or cold.
Slice into strips and add to grains, pastas, vegetables or salads.
Leftovers make great sandwiches. (See photo on page 98)*

Yield: 25 to 30 slices (1/4 inch thick)

Smoke marinade:
- 1 cup soy sauce
- 1/4 cup liquid smoke
- 1/4 cup sugar
- 1 tablespoon salt
- 1 recipe seitan (page 122), or
  - 2 pounds commercial seitan

Mustard marinade:
- 1 tablespoon vegetarian chicken-
  flavored powder
- 1 cup boiling water
- 3/4 cup spicy brown mustard
- 1/2 cup firmly packed brown sugar
- 1 cup vegetable oil
- 1/2 teaspoon ground cloves
- 3 whole garlic cloves, peeled and
  thinly sliced
- Vegetable or olive oil for browning

To make smoke marinade, combine soy sauce, liquid smoke, sugar and salt in a large bowl. Cut seitan on the diagonal into 25 to 30 slices. Add to bowl and marinate 30 minutes. Drain seitan; return to bowl and set aside. Reserve and freeze marinade for later use.

To make mustard marinade, prepare broth by dissolving vegetarian chicken-flavored powder in boiling water. Combine mustard, brown sugar, oil, cloves, vegetarian broth and garlic in blender; emulsify 30 seconds. Pour marinade over seitan; marinate 24 hours.

To serve, brown marinated seitan in vegetable or olive oil over high heat on griddle or in large skillet. For best results, grill seitan over hot coals or hibachi.

Seitan Pastrami

Expand your food horizons with this treasure of culinary ingenuity dreamed up by one of our beloved and eccentric cohorts. In search of the perfect meatless Reuben sandwich, he stumbled upon a blend of herbs and spices that when combined with the seitan mix and baked, results in the flavor and texture of pastrami or salami. An obvious choice for an array of sandwich combinations, this recipe is essential to an antipasto tray.

Yield: one 1¹/₂ pound loaf (14 to 16 slices)

5 dried shiitake mushrooms,*
    stems removed and discarded
1/2 cup hot water

2 tablespoons vegetarian
    beef-flavored powder
1/2 cup boiling water
1 box (12 ounces) seitan mix**
1/4 cup vegetable oil
1/4 cup Worcestershire sauce
1¹/₂ tablespoons minced garlic
1¹/₂ tablespoons whole black
    peppercorns
1¹/₂ tablespoons liquid smoke
1¹/₂ tablespoons whole fennel seeds
1 tablespoon dried oregano,
    crumbled
1 tablespoon dried thyme,
    crumbled
2 teaspoons dried rosemary leaves
1¹/₂ teaspoons salt

Reconstitute shiitakes in hot water for 20 minutes. Drain; discard water. Mince shiitakes.

Prepare broth by dissolving vegetarian beef-flavored powder in boiling water. Combine shiitakes, seitan mix, oil, vegetarian broth, Worcestershire, garlic, peppercorns, liquid smoke, fennel seeds, oregano, thyme, rosemary and salt in large bowl of an electric mixer; knead 15 minutes using paddle attachment. (If electric mixer is not available, knead by hand.)

Preheat oven to 350 degrees F.

Form mixture into a loaf; let rest for 20 minutes. Wrap loaf in foil and bake 45 minutes. Remove foil and bake an additional 15 minutes or until surface starts to brown. Remove from oven and cool completely. Using a serrated knife, slice loaf as thinly as possible (cut on the diagonal to make larger, longer slices). Store in an airtight container.

*Available in Oriental markets.
**Available in natural food markets.

Variation: Omit vegetarian beef-flavored powder and water; replace with 3 tablespoons soy sauce.

Meat Mother

As its name clearly states, this recipe has given birth to a bounty of sensational and savory, yet simple dishes. It is the foundation for all the ground beef ideas found in this book. Just as ground beef is widely acclaimed for its versatility and low cost, so, too, is texturized soy. Inexpensive and non-perishable, it produces excellent meatballs, meat patties, meat loaf, meat pies and on and on. Try some of the recipes contained on the following pages or improvise using Meat Mother as a base.

Yield: 5 cups

1/2 cup vegetarian beef-flavored powder
1¼ cups boiling water
3 cups texturized vegetable protein* (TVP) (page 5)
3 large eggs
1/2 cup solid vegetable shortening
2 tablespoons Kitchen Bouquet
1½ cups bread crumbs
1/2 cup chopped onion
1 tablespoon minced garlic
2 teaspoons dried marjoram, crumbled
2 teaspoons dried thyme, crumbled
1 tablespoon Worcestershire sauce
1/2 cup milk
1 teaspoon coarsely ground black pepper
1 teaspoon salt

Prepare broth in a large bowl by dissolving vegetarian beef-flavored powder in boiling water. Stir in TVP; let stand 2 to 3 minutes. Stir again and let set 1 minute longer. Add eggs, shortening, Kitchen Bouquet, bread crumbs, onion, garlic, marjoram, thyme, Worcestershire, milk, pepper and 1 teaspoon salt or to taste. Mix well by hand, squeezing mixture through fingers to distribute ingredients evenly. Chill or freeze for later use.

Variation: Omit vegetarian beef-flavored powder and water; replace with 1/2 cup soy sauce mixed with 3/4 cup water.

*Available in natural food markets.

Homestyle Meatballs

*This is our contribution to the archives of infinite meatball variations.
Feel free to improvise, perhaps borrowing from the Swedish, Spanish,
French or Greek influences. Serve with any number of sauces including
Marinara Sauce (page 58), Country Gravy (page 53), Mustard Sauce (page 54)
or Barbecue Sauce (page 57). For a spicier flavor, try the I Can't Believe It's
Not Meatballs (page 130). This recipe can be made ahead
and refrigerated or frozen.*

Yield: 24 meatballs

1 recipe (5 cups) Meat Mother
(page 127)

Preheat oven to 400 degrees F.

Roll Meat Mother mixture into 2-inch balls and place on a cookie sheet. For moist meatballs, bake approximately 30 minutes or until a light crust forms. (Do not overbake or meatballs will be dry.)

To freeze, place cooled meatballs on a cookie sheet and put in freezer. When frozen, transfer to a storage container, place waxed paper between layers and return to freezer.

To reheat, deep-fry frozen meatballs for 40 to 60 seconds in vegetable or olive oil. Microwave 1 minute on high for each meatball. To reheat in oven, defrost meatballs and bake 10 to 15 minutes at 350 degrees F until just heated through. Cover with foil to prevent drying.

Meat Loaf

*It doesn't get more basic than this American classic oftentimes
relegated to the ranks of common disdain. At The Cheese Factory,
however, nostalgic memories of mashed potatoes, meat loaf and gravy
are held in high esteem. The virtues of this substantial staple are numerous.
Hot or cold in sandwiches and compatible with practically anything,
this new vintage recipe distinguishes itself in a category all its own.*

Yield: 8 servings

Glaze:
1/2 cup catsup
1/4 cup brown sugar
  1 tablespoon dry mustard

  1 recipe (5 cups) Meat Mother
      (page 127)

Preheat oven to 375 degrees F.

In a small bowl, combine catsup,
brown sugar and mustard. Stir until well
blended.

Line bottom and sides of a 5x9x2 1/2-
inch loaf pan with greased parchment
paper. Place Meat Mother mixture
into pan and smooth top. Make a
shallow groove or depression across
top and fill with glaze. Bake approximately 45 minutes.

I Can't Believe It's Not Meatballs

Here's a story that evokes a chuckle or two. A customer on his first visit to the restaurant proceeded to depart before he had glanced at the menu. When asked if everything was all right, he pointed to a dish of meatballs being served at another table and said, "I'm a vegetarian, and I don't think I can eat here." (The meatballs looked so much like the original, our customer was convinced they were made with ground beef!) We assured him these meatballs contained no meat products and suggested he give them a try. He loved them!
We recommend making the sauce in advance to cut down on preparation time or substituting your favorite commercial red sauce. These meatballs may be prepared several days ahead and reheated in a microwave or moderate 350-degree F oven. They freeze perfectly. Serve on a bed of cooked linguine with plenty of red sauce and freshly grated Parmesan or romano cheese.

Yield: 20 meatballs

1/2 cup vegetarian beef-flavored powder
2 1/2 cups boiling water
5 cups texturized vegetable protein* (TVP) (page 5)
1 cup solid vegetable shortening
5 large eggs
1 cup milk
1 1/2 cups bread crumbs
1 cup grated romano or Parmesan cheese
1/4 cup minced garlic
1 tablespoon salt
1 tablespoon dried thyme, crumbled
2 tablespoons dried basil, crumbled
2 tablespoons dried oregano, crumbled
2 tablespoons chopped fresh Italian parsley
1 tablespoon ground black pepper
3 tablespoons whole fennel seeds
4 tablespoons ground fennel
1 tablespoon ground rosemary
1 1/2 teaspoons red pepper flakes
2 tablespoons Kitchen Bouquet

*Available in natural food markets.

Preheat oven to 400 degrees F.

Prepare broth in a large bowl by dissolving vegetarian beef-flavored powder in boiling water. Stir in TVP; let stand 2 minutes. Stir and let rest another minute until liquid is absorbed. Add shortening, eggs, milk, bread crumbs, romano, garlic, salt, thyme, basil, oregano, parsley, pepper, fennel seeds, ground fennel, rosemary, red pepper flakes and Kitchen Bouquet. Mix well by hand. Shape mixture into 2-inch balls and place in a shallow baking pan. Bake approximately 30 minutes or until a light crust forms. (Meatballs will be moist—do not overbake.)

Variation: Omit beef-flavored vegetarian powder and water; replace with 1/2 cup soy sauce mixed with 2 cups water.

Spicy Italian Red Sauce

Yield: 2 quarts sauce

3 tablespoons olive oil
1/2 cup finely chopped onions
1 tablespoon minced garlic
1/4 cup chopped celery
1/4 cup chopped green pepper
1 teaspoon whole fennel seeds
1 teaspoon red pepper flakes
1/4 cup Burgundy wine
24 ounces (3 cups) canned
   tomato sauce
16 ounces (2 cups) chopped canned
   tomatoes
1 can (12 ounces) tomato juice
1 can (6 ounces) tomato paste
2 tablespoons sugar
1 teaspoon salt
1/2 teaspoon dried oregano,
   crumbled
1/4 teaspoon dried thyme, crumbled
1 teaspoon dried basil, crumbled
1 bay leaf
1 teaspoon ground fennel
1/4 teaspoon ground black pepper
1/2 cup grated Parmesan cheese

To make sauce, heat oil in a heavy-bottomed 4-quart saucepan; add onions, garlic, celery, peppers, fennel seeds and red pepper flakes. Sauté 2 minutes over high heat; add wine, tomato sauce, chopped tomatoes, tomato juice, tomato paste, sugar, salt, oregano, thyme, basil, bay leaf, fennel, pepper and Parmesan. Bring to a boil over medium heat and simmer 30 minutes, stirring occasionally.

Veggie Burgers

These days veggie burgers seem to be the hottest thing since sliced bread, so to speak. Simple and straightforward, this recipe can be augmented with countless components to convey varied taste and texture options. Some possibilities include water chestnuts, assorted toasted nuts, diced carrots, celery, pepper or sautéed mushrooms. Serve on a toasted bun with or without cheese. For condiments and sides, choose from a host of delicious combinations like Barbecue Sauce (page 57), Mustard Sauce (page 54), Guacamole Grande (page 36), salsa and assorted pestos. We recommend making a large batch and freezing.

Yield: 12 veggie burgers

1 recipe (5 cups) Meat Mother (page 127)
1 egg
1/4 cup bread crumbs

Prepare one recipe Meat Mother leaving out 1/4 cup water. Add egg and bread crumbs; mix with hands until well combined. Shape into 12 patties, 1/4 inch thick.

Pan-fry in butter or olive oil 1 minute; or baste with butter and grill over hot coals 1 minute; or brush with butter and bake in moderate 350-degree F oven 1 to 2 minutes. (Remember, this is not meat and does not actually need to be cooked, simply browned and warmed through. Longer cooking will result in a dry, leathery product.)

To freeze, place patties on a cookie sheet in a single layer. When frozen, stack in storage containers placing waxed paper between layers. Return to freezer. To reheat, microwave frozen patty 1 minute on high, then cook as directed above.

Italian Crumble Sausage

*This is the ultimate all-purpose instant enhancer to just about anything.
Make it in large batches and freeze in portions to accommodate everyday
needs. The savory taste and chewy texture complements soups, stews,
chili or marinara sauce. Toss a handful into steamed vegetables and
serve over rice. Great on pizza or in sandwiches (like Sloppy Joes);
it redefines Shepherd's Pie. Mix with leftover rice for stuffing peppers,
eggplant or mushrooms. Toss a handful or two into Savory Corn Bread
Dressing (page 113) for a slightly heartier version. Keeps well in
the refrigerator for one week and freezes perfectly.*

Yield: 6 cups

1/2 cup vegetable shortening
1/3 cup olive oil
1 cup finely chopped onions
1/2 cup chopped green pepper
2 tablespoons minced garlic
1 tablespoon plus 2 teaspoons
   whole fennel seeds
2 tablespoons ground fennel
1 teaspoon red pepper flakes
1 tablespoon plus 1 teaspoon dried
   oregano, crumbled
2 teaspoons dried basil, crumbled
1 teaspoon dried thyme, crumbled
2 teaspoons whole dried rosemary
   leaves, ground in spice grinder
1 tablespoon plus 1 teaspoon
   chopped fresh Italian parsley,
   packed
1 teaspoon coarsely ground
   black pepper
1 teaspoon salt
1/4 cup vegetarian beef-flavored
   powder
1 1/2 cups boiling water
3 cups texturized vegetable
   protein* (TVP) (page 5)

Heat shortening and oil in a 12-inch skillet. Sauté onions, green pepper and garlic for 2 minutes. Add fennel seeds, ground fennel, red pepper flakes, oregano, basil, thyme, rosemary, parsley, pepper and salt. Sauté 1 to 2 minutes more.

Prepare broth in a medium bowl by dissolving vegetarian beef-flavored powder in boiling water; combine with TVP and add to skillet. Stir and simmer until all liquid has been absorbed. Continue to cook over medium heat 3 to 5 minutes or until mixture is lightly browned.

Variation: Omit vegetarian beef-flavored powder and water; replace with 1/2 cup soy sauce mixed with 1 cup water.

*Available in natural food markets.

Adios Gringos Chili

Hearty, robust, pungent, smoky, spicy and sublime!
That's our house chili, and you will love it at your house. Do not be
discouraged by the long list of ingredients. Make it a labor of love and your
efforts will be well rewarded. At the restaurant we serve it with Cheese Factory
Corn Bread (page 112), Charbroiled Vegetables (page 102) or Cactus Salad
(page 80). The chili keeps well in the refrigerator for one week
and freezes perfectly.

Yield: 4 quarts

2 dried chipotle peppers*
1/2 cup hot water
3 tablespoons butter
4 tablespoons shortening
1 cup finely chopped onions
1 tablespoon minced garlic
1/2 cup diced celery
1/2 cup diced green peppers
4 tablespoons corn flour
1 can (46 ounces) tomato juice
16 ounces (2 cups) chopped canned
   tomatoes
32 ounces (4 cups) canned kidney
   beans, drained and rinsed
6 ounces (3/4 cup) canned tomato
   paste
1 tablespoon sugar
2 tablespoons chili powder
1 1/2 teaspoons ground coriander
1 1/2 teaspoons salt
1 teaspoon ground black pepper
1 teaspoon dried thyme, crumbled
1/2 teaspoon ground cinnamon
1/2 teaspoon cayenne pepper
1 tablespoon roasted ground
   cumin (page 13)
2 tablespoons vegetarian beef-
   flavored powder
3/4 cup boiling water
1 1/2 cups texturized vegetable protein**
   (TVP) (page 5)
1/3 cup vegetarian baco bits

*Available in Hispanic markets.
**Available in natural food markets.

Reconstitute chipotle peppers in hot water for 20 minutes. Drain; reserve water. Mince peppers.

In a heavy-bottomed 5-quart soup pot, heat butter and 2 tablespoons of the shortening. Add onion, garlic, celery and green peppers. Sauté over medium-high heat until onion turns translucent. Add remaining 2 tablespoons shortening. Allow shortening to melt and stir in corn flour; combine well with vegetables. Add tomato juice, tomatoes, beans, tomato paste, sugar, chipotle peppers, reserved water, chili powder, coriander, salt, black pepper, thyme, cinnamon, cayenne and cumin. Mix well; reduce heat and simmer 10 to 15 minutes.

Prepare broth in a medium bowl by dissolving vegetarian beef-flavored powder in boiling water. Stir in TVP; mix well and add to chili. Stir in baco bits and simmer another 5 minutes. Garnish individual servings with chopped onion, grated cheese or hot sauce.

Variation: Omit vegetarian beef-flavored powder and water; replace with 2 tablespoons soy sauce mixed with 1/2 cup water.

Tofu Cordon Bleu

*A completely creative composition pays homage to the supreme
versatility of tofu—the backbone of Oriental vegetarian diets.
A stunning orchestration of cheeses enveloped in marinated,
baked, crusty tofu and lightly dowsed with zesty, sweet and
fragrant Orange Tarragon Sauce. For best results, fresh tarragon
is recommended. Serve with Quinoa with Fresh Cilantro (page 115)
or Minted Couscous (page 117).*

Yield: 8 servings

2 cups Orange Tarragon Sauce

2 packages (16 ounces each)
    extra-firm tofu

Orange Tarragon Sauce:
    4 cups orange juice
    2 tablespoons chopped fresh
       tarragon, or 3/4 teaspoon dried
       tarragon, crumbled
    1/2 teaspoon salt
    1 tablespoon butter

Breading:
    4 large eggs
    2 tablespoons half-and-half
    2 cups coarse bread crumbs
    8 tablespoons (24 teaspoons) butter

Filling:
    8 slices (1 ounce each) mozzarella
       cheese
    1 cup bleu cheese, crumbled

Press, stuff-cut, deep-fry and marinate tofu according to package instructions (page 4).

To make sauce, in a 2-quart saucepan, reduce orange juice by half (2 cups) over high heat, stirring occasionally, about 20 minutes. Add tarragon, salt and butter; whisk to blend.

Preheat oven to 500 degrees F.

Using a sharp knife, open each piece of prepared tofu by slicing through 2 sides, leaving 2 sides hinged (equals 8 tofu pouches). (See diagram for stuffed-cut tofu on page 4.) To bread tofu, whisk together eggs and half-and-half in a small bowl. Dip stuffed tofu pouches in egg mixture and dredge in bread crumbs. Stuff tofu by folding 1 slice mozzarella in half and placing inside tofu pouch; then press a little bleu cheese in pouch.

Prepare a 9x13-inch baking pan by placing 16 teaspoons butter (2 teaspoons per pouch) on bottom. Place pouches over butter and dot with remaining 8 teaspoons. Bake 15 to 20 minutes or until golden brown. Serve topped with Orange Tarragon Sauce.

Sweet and Sour Tempeh in Orange Chipotle Sauce

The firm, distinctive texture of tempeh, an Indonesian soy product, combined with the smoky, boldly flavored Orange Chipotle Sauce offers a spicy Southwestern sensation for adventurous palates. Serve with white rice and Spicy Black Beans (page 119), in a flour tortilla or with Cheese Factory Corn Bread (page 112). The sauce may be prepared a day or two ahead (this dish improves with age) and will keep one week in the refrigerator.

Yield: 8 servings tempeh

2 quarts Orange Chipotle Sauce

3 packages (8 ounces each) original soy tempeh*
1/2 cup vegetarian chicken-flavored powder
1 1/2 cups boiling water
3 cups vegetable oil

Orange Chipotle Sauce:
3 tablespoons vegetarian chicken-flavored powder
2 cups boiling water
1 tablespoon minced garlic
2 tablespoons chipotle adobo sauce**
1 whole dried chipotle pepper,** stem removed
1 tablespoon roasted ground cumin (page 13)
1 teaspoon ground fennel seed
1 teaspoon dried oregano, crumbled
1 tablespoon ground coriander
1 tablespoon chili powder
1/2 cup apricot preserves
1/2 cup brown sugar
5 tablespoons cornstarch
1 1/2 cups orange juice
2 tablespoons lemon juice

16 ounces (2 cups) canned plum tomatoes with juice, coarsely chopped
2 teaspoons salt
Zest and juice of 1 orange

1 large red onion (3/4 pound), peeled, cut into 2-inch strips
2 large green peppers (1 pound), seeded, cut into 2-inch strips
2 large red peppers (1 pound), seeded, cut into 2-inch strips

Note: For best results, we use the San Marcos brand of chipotle peppers in adobo sauce.

*Available in natural food markets.
**Available in Hispanic markets.

Cut each piece of tempeh into quarters and each quarter into 2 triangles; place in a large bowl. Prepare broth by dissolving vegetarian chicken-flavored powder in boiling water. Add vegetarian broth to prepared tempeh and marinate overnight. Drain tempeh; pat dry and deep-fry in vegetable oil for 2 minutes or until golden brown on both sides.

To make sauce, prepare broth by dissolving vegetarian chicken-flavored powder in boiling water. Pour into blender; add garlic, chipotle adobo sauce, chipotle pepper, cumin, fennel seed, oregano, coriander, chili powder, apricot preserves and brown sugar.

Purée until ingredients are combined. Transfer to a large saucepan. Dissolve cornstarch in orange juice and add to saucepan. Slowly bring liquid to a boil over medium heat, whisking frequently. Simmer 10 minutes. Add lemon juice, tomatoes, salt, orange zest and juice.

Preheat oven to 400 degrees F. In a 10x12x4-inch baking dish, combine tempeh, sauce, onion and pepper strips. Cover pan with foil and bake 1 hour. Remove from oven and refrigerate 8 hours or overnight. Reheat in a 350-degree F oven for approximately 30 minutes or until warmed through.

Tofu Chicken Paprikash

*This recipe is a meatless interpretation of a Hungarian classic:
a dish of chicken, meat or fish braised with garlic, onions,
sour cream and paprika. Smother the tofu in this subtle, smooth,
savory gravy and serve with hot buttered egg noodles,
mashed potatoes or Gnocchi dí Patate (page 111).
Cwikta—Beet and Horseradish Salad (page 73)
makes a perfect complement to this
Slavic-inspired main course.*

Yield: 8 servings

2 quarts Paprikash Gravy

3 packages (16 ounces each)
   extra-firm tofu

Paprikash Gravy:
  3 tablespoons butter
  3 tablespoons vegetable oil
  2 cups finely chopped onion
  2 teaspoons minced garlic
2 1/2 tablespoons paprika
  1/2 cup vegetarian chicken-flavored
    powder
  4 cups boiling water
  2 cups hot milk
  2 cups flour
  2 cups sour cream
   Salt and ground white pepper
  3 large eggs
  1 tablespoon water
  1 cup flour
  1 teaspoon dried dill, crumbled
  1 teaspoon paprika
   Vegetable shortening for
    frying tofu

Press, chicken-cut, deep-fry and marinate tofu according to instructions (page 3).

To make gravy, heat butter and oil in a heavy-bottomed 4-quart saucepan; add onion and garlic. Sauté over medium-high heat until onion turns translucent; add paprika and cook 30 seconds. Make broth by dissolving vegetarian chicken-flavored powder in boiling water; stir into saucepan. Add milk; bring to a boil and reduce heat to simmer. Combine flour and sour cream in a small bowl; mix well to blend. Add to saucepan; whisk vigorously to incorporate ingredients and prevent lumps from forming. Cook over low heat until sauce is thickened, stirring frequently. (Do not boil.) Remove from heat and adjust seasonings with salt and pepper, as desired.

Beat eggs lightly in a small bowl; add water and stir until well blended. Mix flour, dill and paprika in a separate bowl. Dip pieces of tofu in egg mixture, then flour mixture. Heat shortening in a large skillet; fry tofu on both sides until golden brown. Top individual servings (3 pieces per serving) with Paprikash Gravy.

Stuffed Tofu Parisienne

Participate in an enchanting experience of pure parsnip pleasure, embellished with the velvety texture and smooth richness of a white wine sauce, concealing seasoned tofu baked with Swiss cheese. Serve with Tangy Acorn Squash (page 101), Savory Corn Bread Dressing (page 113) and Cranberry Relish (page 44).

Yield: 8 servings

4 cups Sauce Parisienne

2 packages (16 ounces each) extra-firm tofu

Sauce Parisienne:
12 tablespoons (1 1/2 sticks) butter
1/2 cup flour
1/4 teaspoon salt
2 cups hot milk
3/4 cup white wine

Filling:
1 1/2 sticks butter
3/4 cup finely chopped onion
3/4 cup finely chopped mushrooms
1 1/2 cups shredded parsnips
1 cup cracker crumbs
1/4 cup chopped fresh Italian parsley
3/4 teaspoon salt
1/2 teaspoon ground white pepper
3 tablespoons olive oil
2 cups shredded Swiss cheese
1 teaspoon paprika

Press, chicken-cut, deep-fry and marinate tofu according to instructions (page 3).

To make sauce, melt 6 tablespoons of the butter in a heavy-bottomed 4-quart saucepan over medium heat. Add flour; cook 3 to 4 minutes, stirring constantly until flour begins to darken. Add salt, hot milk, remaining 6 tablespoons butter and wine. Cook over medium heat, whisking frequently until sauce begins to thicken.

To make filling, heat butter in a 12-inch skillet. Add onions and mushrooms. Sauté over high heat 1 to 2 minutes or until onion turns translucent. Add parsnips, cracker crumbs, parsley, 3/4 teaspoon salt or to taste and pepper; mix well.

Using a sharp knife, open each piece of tofu by slicing through 2 sides, leaving remaining 2 sides hinged (equals 8 tofu pouches). (See diagram for stuffed-cut tofu, page 4). Fill pouches generously with filling.

Preheat oven to 400 degrees F.

Brush a 10x12-inch baking pan or individual baking dishes with oil. Place stuffed pouches in pan and cover with sauce. Bake 15 to 20 minutes. Remove from oven; top each serving with 1/4 cup Swiss cheese and a sprinkling of paprika. Return to oven; bake 5 minutes or until cheese has melted. Garnish with fresh parsley sprigs.

Charbroiled Rattlesnake Tofu

*What's in a name?! Those customers outrageous and courageous
enough to order this dish have discovered its unique, smoky, succulent appeal.
This recipe is very simple to prepare and always illicits amusing dining
conversation as well as the sounds of luscious, lusty satisfaction.
Try it with Quinoa with Fresh Cilantro (page 115),
Spicy Black Beans (page 119), Tulsa Salsa (page 39)
and Cactus Salad (page 80).*

Yield: 18 skewers

3 packages (16 ounces each)
   extra-firm tofu
Vegetable oil
1 recipe (1 cup) Western Spice
   (page 57)
1 recipe (3 cups) Barbecue Sauce
   (page 57)

Press, finger-cut, deep-fry and marinate tofu according to instructions (page 3).

Insert an 8- to 9-inch wooden skewer through middle of each tofu piece. Cut each piece at 1/4-inch intervals along 1 side of skewer (see diagram below). Brush sides with oil and dust with Western Spice. Grill over hot coals or broil several minutes until sear marks appear on each piece. Serve with Barbecue Sauce.

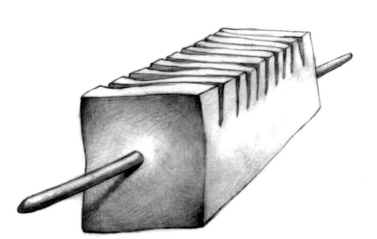

Linguine Primavera with Pesto

*Pasta meals offer a wealth of practical and inexpensive recipes
as well as more elaborate and complex compositions. Adored by young
and old alike, these noodle dishes can be quick to prepare and
afford the cook unlimited creative challenges. Choose from a vast
assortment of commercial or homemade sauces including those
found in this book. This recipe calls for dried linguine
but if you prefer to use fresh pasta, increase the amount of
uncooked pasta by one half (i.e., if the recipe calls for
1 pound dried pasta, use 1½ pounds fresh).*

Yield: 8 servings

1   pound dried linguine
4   tablespoons extra-virgin
      olive oil
2   cups sliced mushrooms
1   large red pepper
      (1/2 pound), seeded and
      julienned
4   large cloves garlic, finely
      minced
1   large zucchini (1/2 pound),
      trimmed, sliced into
      1/4-inch-thick half-moons
2   jars (8 ounces each)
      marinated artichoke
      hearts, quartered
18 to 20   kalamata olives, pitted and
      halved
      Salt and pepper
1   cup Basil Pesto (page 47),
      or favorite commercial
      pesto
      Freshly grated Parmesan
      or romano cheese for
      garnish

Prepare linguine noodles al dente. Heat oil in a 12-inch skillet. Add mushrooms, red pepper and garlic; sauté 2 to 3 minutes. Add zucchini, artichokes and olives; cook 2 more minutes. (Vegetables should be crisp-tender.) Adjust seasonings with salt and pepper, as desired.

Toss linguine with pesto; place on serving platter or in individual dishes. Top with vegetables and freshly grated Parmesan or romano cheese.

Moroccan Shish Kabobs

*Let us entice you with these sensational skewers of marinated
tofu and vegetables. A perfect summertime outdoor barbecue or picnic item,
this recipe will also produce delicious results cooked under a broiler. Use
leftover marinade as a sauce for shish kabobs or as a dressing for vegetables,
pastas and salads. It will keep in the refrigerator for several weeks. Serve shish
kabobs with Minted Couscous (page 117) or Quinoa with Fresh Cilantro (page
115) and Middle Eastern Stuffed Tomatoes (page 18). (See photo on page 91)*

Yield: 16 shish kabobs

4 packages (16 ounces each)
   extra-firm tofu

Marinade:
3 cups olive oil
3/4 cup balsamic vinegar
1/2 cup lemon juice
1/2 cup chopped fresh mint, or
   2 tablespoons dried, crumbled
2 1/2 tablespoons whole dried
   rosemary leaves
1 1/2 tablespoons roasted ground
   cumin (page 13)
3 tablespoons dried oregano,
   crumbled
3 tablespoons salt
1 1/2 tablespoons freshly ground
   black pepper

32 large bay leaves
32 medium-size mushrooms, stems
   removed and discarded
8 large green peppers
2 large onions, peeled, cut into
   1 1/2-inch squares
4 lemons, cut into eighths
8 roma tomatoes, cut into eighths

Press, skewer-cut, deep-fry and marinate tofu according to instructions (page 3).

To make marinade, combine oil, vinegar, lemon juice, mint, rosemary, cumin, oregano, salt and pepper in a medium bowl; set aside. Soak bay leaves in marinade until ready to assemble shish kabobs; set aside.

Wipe mushrooms clean with damp paper towel. Cut both ends off peppers and slice in half lengthwise. Remove seeds and membrane. Cut each half into 4 squares (yields 8 squares per pepper).

Grill mushrooms over hot coals or under broiler until just softened. Remove from heat and set aside. Grill or broil pepper pieces 2 to 3 minutes until just blackened. Remove from heat and set aside. Grill or broil onion pieces until opaque and softened. Remove from heat and set aside. Remove bay leaves from marinade.

On a skewer (metal, bamboo or wood, approximately 10 inches long), thread lemon wedge, bay leaf, green pepper square, tofu chunk, 2 onion squares, tomato wedge, mushroom, green pepper square and tofu chunk (tofu will be in center). Continue to thread with green pepper square, mushroom, tomato wedge, 2 onion squares, tofu chunk, green pepper square, bay leaf and lemon (this is a mirror-image of first half). Place skewers in large shallow pan in single layer. Pour marinade over skewers and marinate 30 minutes. Remove from marinade; grill skewers over hot coals or under broiler several minutes until tomatoes start to shrivel.

Luscious Lasagna

Three layers of a perfectly integrated blend of ingredients result in sublime satisfaction. This casserole is assembled using uncooked lasagna noodles. Yes, it's true! Simply place four layers of uncooked noodles between the ingredients listed below, and voila! We recommend making the spinach filling and marinara a day or two ahead to cut down on preparation time. Or, if preferred, use a favorite commercial marinara. This triple decker dish is a guaranteed crowd-pleaser. It keeps well in the refrigerator for one week, freezes perfectly and reheats in a microwave or moderate 350-degree F oven.

Yield: 8 servings

Spinach-mushroom filling:
  3 pounds frozen chopped spinach, thawed and drained
  4 tablespoons olive oil
1 1/2 cups finely chopped onion
  2 teaspoons minced garlic
  1 teaspoon dried oregano, crumbled
  1 teaspoon dried thyme, crumbled
  1 teaspoon dried basil, crumbled
1 1/2 pounds sliced mushrooms (7 cups)
  1 teaspoon salt

Ricotta filling:
  3 cups ricotta cheese
  3 large eggs
  1 teaspoon minced garlic
  1 teaspoon ground fennel

White sauce:
  1 cup (2 sticks) unsalted butter
  1 cup flour
  2 quarts milk
  2 bay leaves
  1/8 teaspoon ground nutmeg
  Salt and pepper

1 cup good-quality grated Parmesan cheese
1 cup good-quality grated romano cheese
1 pound uncooked lasagna noodles
5 cups shredded mozzarella cheese (1 1/4 pounds)
1 1/2 cups thinly sliced fresh basil
1 recipe (2 quarts) Marinara Sauce (page 58), or 2 quarts commercial marinara sauce

To make spinach filling, place spinach in a clean towel and squeeze out excess moisture. Heat oil in a 12-inch skillet; add onion, garlic, oregano, thyme and basil. Sauté 1 to 2 minutes over high heat until onion turns translucent. Add mushrooms; cook for another minute. Add spinach and salt. Reduce heat to medium and cook until most of the liquid has evaporated. Remove from heat and set aside.

To make ricotta filling, combine ricotta, eggs, garlic and fennel in a medium bowl; refrigerate until needed.

To make white sauce, melt butter in a heavy-bottomed 4-quart saucepan. Whisk in flour to form a roux. Cook roux over low heat 3 minutes, stirring frequently. Heat milk and add to roux; whisk vigorously to avoid lumps. Add bay leaves; bring to a boil over low heat, whisk continuously. When sauce is smooth and begins to thicken, remove from heat. Discard bay leaves and add nutmeg. Adjust seasonings with salt and pepper, as desired. (White sauce should be warm to facilitate easy pouring. If prepared ahead of time, reheat in microwave or double boiler.) Combine Parmesan and romano cheeses.

Preheat oven to 400 degrees F.

In a 10x12x4-inch casserole dish, cover bottom with 1 1/2 cups of the white sauce; add a single layer of the noodles. Continue layering with 1 cup of the ricotta filling, 1 cup of the mozzarella, 1/2 cup of the basil, 1/2 cup of the cheese mixture and 1/3 of the spinach mixture. Repeat process in the same order for second and third layers. Complete dish by placing 1 3/4 cups of the white sauce, single layer of remaining noodles and remaining 1 3/4 cups white sauce over top. Cover with foil and bake 45 to 60 minutes. Remove foil and sprinkle remaining 2 cups mozzarella over top. Bake uncovered an additional 3 to 4 minutes or until cheese is melted and slightly browned. Let stand 15 to 20 minutes before serving. Serve on a pool of marinara sauce.

Paradise Pasta with Tropical Fruit Sauce

A sauce is a sure way to draw the elements of a dish together. The allure of this Polynesian-inspired delicacy resides in an artful integration of flavors. If you are in the mood for something luscious and exotic, the vibrant hues and intriguing nuances of this Hawaiian concoction will tease and tantalize your taste buds. The sauce can be made in advance and reheated in a microwave or double boiler. It keeps well in the refrigerator for five days.

Yield: 8 servings

2 quarts Tropical Fruit Sauce

1 bag (10 ounces) frozen
  raspberries, thawed

Tropical Fruit Sauce:
  4 teaspoons butter
  2 teaspoons minced garlic
  2 cans (12 ounces each)
    Goya Guava Nectar*
  2 pints heavy cream
  4 teaspoons dried tarragon,
    crumbled
  1/3 cup cornstarch
  1 teaspoon salt
  1/2 teaspoon ground white pepper
  1 teaspoon orange zest
  1 can (11 ounces) mandarin
    orange sections, drained

48 cheese-filled ravioli
    (fresh or frozen)
  4 firm bananas
  3 tablespoons butter
  2 tablespoons brown sugar
    Juice of 1 lemon
  8 large fresh strawberries,
    cut in half lengthwise
  8 sprigs fresh mint

*Available in Hispanic or specialty food markets.

Place raspberries in a food processor and process until smooth. Transfer raspberry purée to small sieve and strain seeds; reserve 3 tablespoons purée for sauce. Freeze remaining sauce for later use or use in Fruit Vinaigrette (page 87).

To make sauce, heat butter in a heavy-bottomed 4-quart saucepan. Add garlic; sauté 30 seconds over medium heat. Add 1 can of the guava nectar; stir in cream. Heat gently until liquid is hot, but not boiling. Add tarragon and stir. Dissolve cornstarch with remaining can of guava nectar; add to hot liquid, whisk briskly and continuously until mixture thickens. (Do not allow to boil.) Simmer 2 to 3 minutes; whisking vigorously. Remove from heat; add reserved raspberry purée, salt, pepper and orange zest. Just before serving add mandarin orange sections.

Cook ravioli in a large kettle of boiling water according to package instructions.

Peel and slice bananas in half lengthwise, then in half horizontally (4 pieces from each banana). Heat butter in a 12-inch skillet; sauté bananas 1 minute over high heat. Sprinkle with brown sugar and lemon juice; set aside.

To serve, ladle a generous amount of sauce onto center of plate; arrange 6 ravioli around edge and place 2 banana slices in center. Garnish with strawberries and mint.

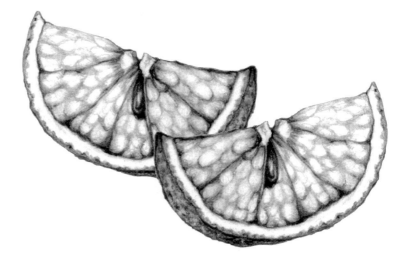

Chilled Sesame Noodles

The impact of this Oriental noodle dish is pleasingly potent.
Steeped in deep, golden sesame alchemy and heightened with fresh gingerroot,
lemon and cilantro, this recipe promises perfect picnic fare or light main course
possibilities. Rice noodles or Japanese udon noodles can be used for variation;
delicious with Mandarin Lettuce Salad (page 82). It keeps well in the
refrigerator three to four days and is a good leftover meal to have on hand.

Yield: 4 quarts noodles

3/4 cup sweetened, shredded coconut

Dressing:
1/2 cup dark sesame oil
1/2 cup tamari or soy sauce
1/4 cup Tamarind Ginger Garlic
       Sauce (page 160), or
       commercial hoisin sauce
1 tablespoon minced garlic
1 tablespoon minced fresh
       gingerroot
1/4 cup lemon juice

11/2 pounds dried linguine, cooked
       al dente and chilled
1/2 cup chopped fresh cilantro,
       packed
1 cup thinly sliced scallions
1 large carrot (1/2 pound), peeled
       and thinly julienned
1/4 cup toasted sesame seeds
       (page 12)
1 recipe Smoked Eggs with Citrus
       Herb Sauce (8 eggs, page 31)
       (optional)

Toast coconut in a dry skillet over medium heat; stir frequently until golden colored (2 to 3 minutes). Remove from heat and cool.

To make dressing, combine oil, soy sauce, Tamarind Sauce, garlic, gingerroot and lemon juice in a small bowl; whisk to incorporate.

Combine linguine, cilantro, scallions and carrots in a large bowl; toss with dressing. Garnish with a sprinkling of sesame seeds and toasted coconut. For garnishing individual plates, add 1 Smoked Egg, quartered and arrange around edge.

Chili Rellenos

(Chili Peppers Stuffed with Jack Cheese)

*The poblano, a large Mexican dark green, mild-tasting chili pepper,
is recommended for this recipe. Fuel your lusty Latin passions
with a rich and cheesy baked casserole dish which begs to be served
with Sweet and Sassy Salsa (page 43), Mexican "Ouchies" (page 79),
Spicy Black Beans (page 119) and Quinoa with Fresh Cilantro (page 115).*

Yield: 9 stuffed peppers

9 large poblano peppers*
   (3 ounces each)
2 tablespoons vegetable oil
2 pounds Monterey Jack cheese,
   shredded
5 large eggs
1 1/4 cups whole milk
1/4 cup flour
1/2 teaspoon salt
1/4 teaspoon ground black pepper
1/2 pound Cheddar cheese, shredded

Preheat oven to 450 degrees F.

Rub peppers with oil and place on a rack over a shallow baking pan. Roast 10 to 12 minutes; turn peppers over and continue roasting an additional 10 minutes or until skins begin to char and crack. (Flesh should be tender, but remain firm enough to hold stuffing.) Place hot peppers into a container; seal and steam for 1 hour. (This will facilitate removal of skins and seeds.)

Make a slit on 1 side of each pepper (pepper must remain whole to stuff). Peel away skins and remove seeds and membranes. Stuff each pepper with Jack cheese and place seam side down in a 9x13-inch baking pan or in individual baking dishes.

Preheat oven to 350 degrees F.

In a large bowl, mix eggs, milk, flour, salt and pepper; pour over stuffed peppers. Bake 15 to 20 minutes or until egg sets (individual baking dishes require less time). Top with Cheddar and bake an additional 4 to 5 minutes. Remove from oven; let stand 10 minutes before serving.

*Available in the specialty produce section of local supermarkets or Hispanic markets.

Crêpes Champignons

The mild, delicate flavor and commendable tenderness of crêpes combine so agreeably with almost any other food, that it is a piece of cake to come up with imaginative new ways to serve them. This dish is undoubtedly rich and is good to combine with the refreshing character of a crisp tossed salad. Any number of alternative fillings may be used; seasoned spinach, freshly steamed asparagus and ratatouille are some good ones. Assorted fruit fillings also make great dessert crêpes. The crêpes and fillings can be prepared a day or two ahead and assembled and reheated just before serving. Leftover mushroom filling makes a terrific pasta sauce. (See photo on page 92)

Yield: 35 to 40 crêpes

2^1/2 quarts mushroom filling

Crêpes:
- 6 large eggs
- 1^1/3 cups milk
- 2/3 cup half-and-half
- 1 cup water
- 1 teaspoon salt
- 2 cups flour
- 2 tablespoons butter, melted
- 2 tablespoons sugar
- 1/4 cup brandy
- 1 tablespoon butter

Mushroom filling:
- 6^1/2 cups whole milk
- 3 cups dried shiitake mushrooms*
  (2^1/2 ounces), stems removed
  and discarded
- 2 bay leaves
- 8 tablespoons butter
- 3/4 cup finely chopped onion
- 3 pounds sliced white button
  mushrooms
- 1^1/2 tablespoons brandy
- 3/4 cup flour
- 1 teaspoon grated nutmeg
- 1 tablespoon salt
- 3/4 teaspoon ground white pepper

Mushroom sauce:
- 3 cups mushroom filling
- 1/2 cup reserved
  shiitake-flavored milk
- 1 cup whole milk
- 1/2 teaspoon salt
- 8 to 12 whole white button
  mushrooms, medium to
  large with 1/2-inch stems
- 1 tablespoon butter

*Available in Asian and Oriental markets.

To make crêpes, combine eggs, milk, half-and-half, water, salt, flour, melted butter, sugar and brandy in blender. Chill in refrigerator at least 2 hours or overnight. Heat a 7-inch crêpe or non-stick omelette pan; add 1 tablespoon butter and swirl mixture evenly to coat pan. When foam subsides, pour 3 tablespoons batter into pan (a 1¹/2-ounce ladle holds 3 tablespoons liquid). Tilt pan quickly to spread batter evenly. Cook over medium heat for about 1 minute. Loosen edge of crêpe with rubber spatula and flip or turn crêpe over with fingers. Cook about 1 minute longer or until golden spots appear throughout crêpe. (The first few may be a little ragged, but as confidence is developed and heat is adjusted, results will improve dramatically.) Continue making crêpes, brushing pan with melted butter before adding batter.

To make filling, place milk, shiitakes and bay leaves in a 4-quart saucepan; heat slowly until almost boiling. Remove from heat. Cover and set aside for 20 minutes. Strain shiitakes and discard bay leaves; reserve shiitake-flavored milk. Mince shiitakes in a food processor using metal blade attachment.

Heat 2 tablespoons of the butter in a 12-inch skillet; sauté onions until translucent. Add sliced mushrooms and cook over high heat, stirring frequently until most of the water has evaporated. Add shiitakes and brandy; cook 1 to 2 minutes. Remove from heat and set aside.

Melt remaining 6 tablespoons butter in a 5-quart saucepan. Add flour and whisk vigorously. Cook 2 minutes; stir constantly. Add all but ¹/2 cup reserved shiitake-flavored milk and whisk vigorously to incorporate flour. Add nutmeg and bring to a gentle boil over medium heat; whisk until thickened. Cook 2 to 3 minutes longer; add mushroom mixture and stir until well blended. Adjust seasonings with salt and pepper, as desired.

To make sauce, purée 3 cups mushroom filling, reserved ¹/2 cup shiitake milk, whole milk and ¹/2 teaspoon salt or to taste in a blender until smooth. Transfer to a small saucepan and warm over low heat. Wipe mushrooms clean with damp paper towel and slice ¹/8 inch thick. Heat butter in a small skillet; sauté mushroom slices until tender, reserving large slices from center of mushrooms for garnish.

Fold crêpes in half and then in half again, so that each is shaped like a triangle. Fill top fold with 1 heaping tablespoon mushroom filling and place in serving dish. Cover and reheat gently in a moderate 350-degree F oven until just warmed through. Stuffed crêpes may also be reheated in microwave. To serve, place 3 to 5 crêpes on each plate; spoon sauce over bottom half of each crêpe, leaving filled end exposed. Garnish with mushroom slice.

Leek Tart with Chèvre

*Leeks have a mild almost sweet flavor that is all their own. In Europe,
leeks are plentiful and cheap and are called "the asparagus of the poor."
They are still a favorite first course, served hot or cold, in French bistros.
Savory and delicious, the marriage of leeks and goat cheese graces any table
with rustic elegance. This tart makes an appealing presentation (see cover
photo) on a brunch buffet or served as a light luncheon entrée with Middle
Eastern Stuffed Tomatoes (page 18) and Grilled Garlic Mushrooms (page 109).*

Yield: 6 entrées or 12 appetizers

Pastry dough:
2 1/4 cups flour
   1 teaspoon salt
   8 tablespoons butter, chilled
   3 tablespoons vegetable shortening
  1/2 cup ice water

Leek filling:
   3 small leeks (12 ounces)
     (10 inches long)
   1 tablespoon butter
   1 teaspoon minced garlic
   1 teaspoon dried dill, crumbled
   4 tablespoons half-and-half
  1/8 teaspoon ground nutmeg
  1/4 teaspoon salt

Custard filling:
   1 cup milk
   3 large eggs
   6 ounces fresh chèvre
   1 teaspoon Worcestershire sauce
  1/4 teaspoon salt

To make pastry, combine flour and salt in a medium bowl. Working quickly, cut butter into thin slices; add sliced butter and shortening to flour mixture. Using fingertips, swiftly incorporate ingredients until mixture resembles coarse meal. Drizzle ice water over mixture and form into a ball. (Do not knead dough; compact with hands.) Wrap in waxed paper and chill 1 hour.

Place dough on a floured work surface. Using a rolling pin, flatten into a circle (1 inch thick by 6 inches in diameter). Roll dough from center to form an even circle (1/8 inch thick by 14 inches in diameter). Place dough in a 10 1/2 x1-inch round quiche pan with removable bottom. Trim edges and prick bottom of dough with fork. (Tart shell may be frozen at this time for later use.)

Preheat oven to 400 degrees F. Cut and fit a sheet of parchment paper on top of prepared dough. Place a 9 1/2-inch round pan in center to act as a weight. Bake approximately 15 minutes or until crust is firm, but not brown. Remove baking pan and paper; cool pastry on wire rack.

To make leek filling, trim roots and 1 inch of green from leeks. Cut in half lengthwise and rinse to remove sand or grit. Reserve 1 half length for garnish.

Thinly slice remaining leeks horizontally to obtain 3 cups (lightly packed). Separate leaves of reserved leek and plunge into skillet of boiling water for 1 to 2 minutes. Remove from pan and immerse in ice water to stop cooking. Drain and pat dry; set aside.

Heat butter in a 10-inch skillet; add leeks and garlic. Sauté over medium-high heat until leeks begin to wilt. Add dill and cook 1 minute longer. Add half-and-half, nutmeg and salt; cook over medium heat until cream has been absorbed and leeks are tender.

To make custard, combine milk, eggs, goat cheese, Worcestershire and salt in food processor; process 30 seconds.

Preheat oven to 375 degrees F. Spoon leek filling into baked crust. Gently pour custard over filling and garnish with reserved leeks (see photo on cover). Bake approximately 40 minutes or until filling is set and pastry is browned. Remove from oven and brush with a small amount of oil to keep surface from drying out. (Allow tart to cool 15 minutes before serving or serve at room temperature.)

Spanikopita

*One bite of this subtly seasoned spinach pie will instantly transport you
to the sunny beaches of Greece from whence hails this delectable filled pastry.
Enhance the illusion by serving it with Mediterranean Rice (page 114),
Melidzanes Salata (page 75) or Middle Eastern Stuffed Tomatoes (page 18).
If you have never worked with phyllo dough, fear not.
Simply follow the directions in this recipe
for guaranteed splendid results.*

Yield: 8 servings

1 cup (2 sticks) butter,
　approximately
4 tablespoons olive oil
2 cups finely chopped onion
1/2 teaspoon minced garlic
1/2 teaspoon dried basil, crumbled
1/2 teaspoon dried oregano,
　crumbled
1/2 teaspoon salt
1/2 teaspoon ground black pepper
1/8 teaspoon cayenne pepper
2 large eggs
1/2 cup heavy cream
1/8 teaspoon ground nutmeg
3 pounds frozen chopped spinach,
　thawed and drained
1/2 pound Cheddar cheese, shredded
1 pound feta cheese, crumbled
1 1/2 packages phyllo dough*
　(30 sheets)
1 tablespoon sesame seeds

*Available in frozen food section of
supermarkets.

Heat 1 tablespoon of the butter and 1
tablespoon of the oil in a 12-inch skillet; sauté onion and garlic over
medium heat until onion turns translucent. Add basil, oregano, salt, black
pepper and cayenne; cook 1 minute
longer. Remove from heat and set
aside.

Lightly beat eggs in a large bowl. Add
cream and nutmeg; stir well to combine. Place spinach in a clean towel
and squeeze out excess moisture; add
to egg mixture. Add onion mixture,
Cheddar and feta; mix well by hand.

Melt remaining butter and add to
remaining oil in a small bowl; set aside
for brushing pastry.

Preheat oven to 325 degrees F.

Carefully read handling instructions
on package of phyllo. (The dough is
paper thin and dries out quickly. Cover
with a damp cloth while working, and
do not be concerned if it cracks or
breaks; it is very forgiving. Simply
brush dough with melted butter, patch
pieces together and continue.)

Using a pastry brush, butter bottom
and sides of a 15x9 1/2x2-inch glass
baking dish. Line bottom, sides and
ends of dish using 2 sheets of phyllo
for each; leave a 3-inch overhang of
dough around dish. Generously brush
pastry with butter mixture, especially

the overhang. Work quickly; repeat process, adding 2 more layers using 2 sheets phyllo per layer (6 sheets per side=total of 24 sheets). (Make sure to generously brush between each sheet and the overhang with butter mixture during assembly.)

Spoon spinach mixture evenly into pan. Layer 6 sheets phyllo over top, brushing each sheet with butter mixture. Roll overhang of dough down into pan (one side at a time) to resem-

ble pie crust and to give casserole a finished appearance. (Phyllo along sides may be very brittle at this stage; brush generously with butter mixture to moisten to allow for easier handling.) Use a serrated knife, cutting only through top layers of phyllo, to score pie into 8 servings. Sprinkle with sesame seeds and bake 35 to 40 minutes until crust is golden brown. Remove from oven; rest 10 to 15 minutes before serving.

Katchapuri with Roasted Vegetables and Wisconsin Herbed Goat Cheese

Russian in origin, Katchapuri is a yeast bread made with milk and butter and traditionally filled with layers of spinach, cheese and salmon. Here is an adaptation using eggplant, roasted peppers, zucchini and fresh goat cheese. This dish is visually stunning and a feast for the eyes as well as the palate. The filling ingredients should be prepared a day ahead and refrigerated. Serve the Katchapuri warm or at room temperature with a tossed salad and cup of steaming Zucchini Basil Soup (page 67).

Yield: 8 entrées

16 appetizers

2 red peppers (12 ounces)
2 yellow peppers (12 ounces)
2 tablespoons olive oil

Pepper marinade:
2 tablespoons balsamic vinegar
3 tablespoons olive oil
1 tablespoon minced garlic
1 teaspoon dried thyme, crumbled
1/2 teaspoon salt
1/2 teaspoon ground black pepper

Roasted vegetables:
1 eggplant (1 1/4 pounds)
1 onion (1/2 pound)
1 zucchini (9 ounces)
2 tablespoons olive oil
2 teaspoons minced garlic
1/2 teaspoon salt
1/2 teaspoon ground black pepper
1 teaspoon dried basil, crumbled
1 teaspoon dried oregano, crumbled

Dough:
2 packages (1/4 ounce each) active dry yeast
1 1/2 teaspoons sugar
1 cup lukewarm milk (110 to 115 degrees F)
3 1/2 to 4 cups flour
2 teaspoons salt
1/2 cup (1 stick) butter, softened
1 large egg
2 tablespoons cold water
3 ounces Swiss cheese, shredded
4 tablespoons kalamata olives, pitted and quartered lengthwise
12 ounces herbed goat cheese, cut into bite-size chunks
2 tablespoons sesame seeds

Preheat oven to 450 degrees F. Rub peppers with oil and place on a rack over a shallow baking pan. Roast 15 to 20 minutes; turn peppers over and continue roasting an additional 20 minutes or until skins begin to char and crack and peppers collapse. (The flesh should remain tender but firm, not mushy.) To maintain the bright color of the peppers, be careful not to allow them to darken too much. Place hot peppers into a container; seal and steam for 1 hour. (This will facilitate removal of the skins and seeds.)

To make marinade, combine vinegar, oil, garlic, thyme, salt and pepper in a small bowl; whisk to incorporate ingredients. Remove skins and seeds from peppers and discard. Add peppers to marinade and refrigerate 24 hours.

To roast vegetables, trim stem and bottom off eggplant and discard. Cut into 1-inch cubes. Peel and cut onion into 1-inch squares, separating layers. Trim ends of zucchini, quarter lengthwise and cut into 3/4-inch-thick pieces. Combine oil, garlic, salt, pepper, basil and oregano; toss with eggplant and onions in a large bowl. Preheat oven to 400 degrees F. Place eggplant and onions on a cookie sheet in a single layer. Bake 20 minutes; add zucchini and bake an additional 5 minutes. Remove from oven and cool.

To make dough, sprinkle yeast and 1/2 teaspoon of the sugar over 1/2 cup of the milk in a small, shallow bowl. Stir and set aside in a warm, draft-free spot until mixture has doubled in volume. Pour 3 cups of the flour into a large bowl and make a deep well in center. Add remaining 1/2 cup milk, yeast mixture, remaining 1 teaspoon sugar, salt and butter. Mix ingredients together with hands, shaping dough into a ball. (An electric mixer with a dough hook attachment works well for preparation of dough.) Place on lightly floured surface and knead 10 minutes or until dough is smooth and elastic. Place dough in a large lightly greased bowl and cover with a kitchen towel. Let dough rise in a warm spot for about 45 minutes to 1 hour or until doubled in bulk. Punch down and set aside to rise another 30 to 40 minutes or until dough again doubles in bulk. (Make sure filling ingredients are ready and on hand.)

Preheat oven to 375 degrees F. Prepare egg wash by beating egg and cold water lightly with a fork; set aside. Remove and drain roasted peppers from marinade; set aside.

Punch down dough and place on a floured surface. Roll out to form a large circle (26 inches in diameter). (Dough is very elastic and will stretch easily; use enough flour for dusting to keep dough from sticking to work surface.) Gently lift dough, wrap around rolling pin and fit into a greased and floured 91/2-inch springform pan. (Several inches of dough should hang over sides of pan.)

Line bottom of pan with Swiss cheese and place half the eggplant mixture over cheese. Sprinkle half of the olives and half of the goat cheese evenly over surface and line with red pepper pieces. Layer with remaining eggplant mixture, olives, goat cheese and yellow peppers; distribute evenly. Draw excess dough over filling. Rotate pan and pleat into loose folds. Gather ends of dough together in center and twist into a small knot. Brush loaf with egg wash; sprinkle with sesame seeds. Set loaf aside to rest 10 minutes. Bake approximately 1 hour or until loaf is golden brown. Remove from oven; cool on wire rack 30 minutes and release springform pan. To serve, cut into 8 wedges for entrées, 16 wedges for appetizers; serve warm or at room temperature.

Mixed Vegetables with Thai Coconut Peanut Curry Sauce

At The Cheese Factory, we've greeted world travelers dedicated to the pursuit of international dining. Their comments on this particular dish have been unanimously enthusiastic. You are invited to sample the splendid authentic flavors of this main course served with Asian rice. The mildly spicy version presented here may be adjusted by increasing or reducing the amount of red curry paste. The sauce can be prepared ahead and refrigerated or frozen for later use.

Yield: 8 servings

2 quarts Thai Coconut Peanut Curry Sauce

1 package (16 ounces) extra-firm tofu

Thai Coconut Peanut Curry Sauce:
2 cups creamy peanut butter
4 tablespoons peanut oil
3 tablespoons Thai red curry paste*
3 tablespoons vegetarian chicken-flavored powder
6 cups boiling water
1 tablespoon salt
2 cans (15 ounces each) coconut cream**
4 tablespoons cornstarch
1/2 cup cold water

Asian rice:
6 cups jasmine rice*
2 1/2 teaspoons salt
9 cups cold water

Vegetables:
6 tablespoons peanut oil
1 pound onions, peeled, thinly sliced (4 cups)
1 pound carrots, peeled, cut into matchsticks (4 cups)
12 ounces mushrooms, thinly sliced (4 cups)
40 whole fresh basil leaves (1 to 2 bunches)
1 pound zucchini, sliced in half lengthwise, then diagonally into 1/2-inch-thick half-moons
24 ounces (3 cups) canned bamboo shoots, drained and rinsed
1/2 cup toasted coconut
1 can (11 ounces) mandarin orange sections, drained

*Available in Asian and Oriental markets.
**Available in liquor department of local supermarket or liquor store.

Press, oriental-cut, deep-fry and marinate tofu according to instructions (page 4).

To make sauce, combine peanut butter, oil and curry paste in a heavy-bottomed 4-quart saucepan. Prepare broth by dissolving vegetarian chicken-flavored powder in boiling water; add to saucepan. Add salt and coconut cream; mix well. Bring to a boil over medium-high heat, stirring often with a wire whisk. Reduce heat to simmer. Dissolve cornstarch with cold water in a small bowl; stir into sauce. Simmer until sauce thickens, whisking constantly. Remove from heat; use immediately, refrigerate or freeze for later use. Reheat in microwave or double boiler.

To make rice, combine jasmine rice, salt and cold water in a heavy-bottomed 4-quart saucepan with tight-fitting lid; bring to a boil. Reduce heat to simmer and cook approximately 15 minutes or until water has been absorbed, and rice is tender. Turn heat off and allow rice to steam covered for an additional 10 minutes.

To prepare vegetables, heat oil in a large wok or skillet. Add onions, carrots and mushrooms; cook 2 to 3 minutes over high heat until onion begins to wilt. Add basil, zucchini, bamboo shoots and tofu; cook another 2 minutes. (Vegetables should remain crisp-tender.) Vegetables may be stir-fried in 2 to 3 batches, as necessary. Transfer cooked vegetables to a large bowl and mix with warm Thai sauce (approximately 6 to 8 ounces per serving). Serve on a bed of Asian rice. Garnish with a sprinkling of toasted coconut and several mandarin orange sections.

Oriental Stir-Fry with
Tamarind Ginger Garlic Sauce

*Do not be dissuaded by unfamiliar ingredients in this recipe. Trying something
totally different is part of the excitement and fun of cooking as it is in life.
Your efforts will be well rewarded with the results of this spectacular collection
of intricate Oriental flavors and textures. The sauce may be prepared ahead and
reheated. It keeps well in the refrigerator for two weeks and can be frozen.
Freezing may cause a breakdown in the consistency of the sauce;
purée in a blender to return to desired, smooth texture.*

Yield: 10 servings

Asian rice:
    6 cups jasmine rice*
 2¹/2 teaspoons salt
    9 cups cold water

Tamarind Ginger Garlic Sauce:
    4 dried tamarind pods*
    1 dried tangerine peel*
    1 cup hot water
 1¹/2 cups soy sauce
  ¹/4 cup minced garlic
    4 teaspoons minced fresh
        gingerroot
 1¹/2 teaspoons galanga*
    2 cups packed brown sugar
    3 tablespoons vegetarian
        chicken-flavored powder
 4¹/2 cups boiling water
  ²/3 cup apricot preserves
 6¹/2 tablespoons peanut oil
    1 tablespoon plus 2 teaspoons
        dark sesame oil*
    1 tablespoon plus 2 teaspoons
        Chinese hot oil*
 2¹/2 teaspoons Chinese chili
        powder*
10¹/2 tablespoons cornstarch
    1 cup cold water

Vegetables:
    6 tablespoons peanut oil
    2 cups thinly sliced onions
    3 cups carrots, cut into matchsticks
    2 cups celery, thinly sliced on the
        diagonal
    2 cups sliced mushrooms
    2 cups canned baby corn,
        drained and rinsed
   24 snow peas, ends trimmed
    1 medium head bok choy,
        cut into 1-inch pieces
    1 can (8 ounces) whole water
        chestnuts, drained and rinsed

Garnish:
    Toasted cashews (page 12)
    Toasted sesame seeds (page 12)
    Seasoned tofu (oriental-cut)
        (page 4)

*Available in Asian or Oriental
markets.

To prepare rice, combine rice, salt and cold water in a 6-quart heavy-bottomed saucepan with tight-fitting lid. Bring to a boil over high heat; reduce heat to simmer and cook approximately 15 minutes or until water has been absorbed and rice is tender. Turn heat off and allow rice to steam covered for an additional 10 minutes.

To make sauce, soak tamarind pods and tangerine peel in hot water for 20 minutes. Drain; reserve water and finely mince. Prepare broth by dissolving vegetarian chicken-flavored powder with boiling water. In a heavy-bottomed 4-quart saucepan, combine minced tamarind and tangerine, reserved water, soy sauce, garlic, gingerroot, galanga, brown sugar and 4 cups of the vegetarian broth.

In blender, combine remaining 1/2 cup vegetarian broth with preserves; purée and add to saucepan. Add peanut oil, sesame oil, Chinese hot oil and chili powder. Bring to a boil over high heat; reduce heat to simmer. Mix cornstarch with cold water and stir into saucepan. Reduce heat to low and simmer until sauce thickens and vegetables are ready. (Sauce may be refrigerated or frozen for later use.)

To stir-fry vegetables, heat oil in a large wok or skillet. Add onions, carrots, celery and mushrooms; cook 2 to 3 minutes over high heat until onion begins to wilt. Add baby corn, snow peas, bok choy and water chestnuts; cook an additional 2 minutes. (Vegetables should remain crisp-tender and may be stir-fried in 2 to 3 batches, as necessary.) Transfer cooked vegetables to a large bowl; mix with warm sauce (4 to 6 ounces per serving). Serve with Asian rice and garnish with toasted cashews, sesame seeds or tofu.

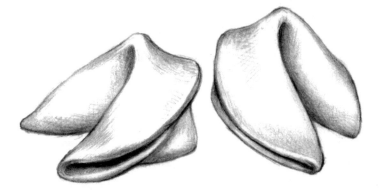

Mushroom Potato Stroganoff

*Many of our most popular dishes hail from a colorful
European heritage and have been adapted by our staff to
accommodate availability of ingredients and ease of preparation.
This recipe certainly captures the essence of a classic
stroganoff with a few unexpected surprises.
Try it with Honeyed Apples Stuffed
with Red Cabbage (page 104).*

Yield: 3 quarts

3/4 cup whole milk
1 bay leaf
1/4 cup dried shiitake mushrooms*
    (1/2 ounce), stems removed
    and discarded
1 large potato, peeled and diced
    into 1/4-inch cubes
1 pound white button mushrooms
4 tablespoons butter
1 1/2 cups finely chopped onion
1 tablespoon minced garlic
1/3 cup flour
1/3 cup Burgundy wine
1 cup water
1 tablespoon vegetarian beef-
    flavored powder or soy sauce
1/3 cup tomato juice
2 tablespoons Worcestershire
    sauce
2 teaspoons salt
1 teaspoon ground white pepper
1 cup sour cream
1/2 teaspoon ground nutmeg
1 teaspoon paprika

Heat milk and bay leaf in a small saucepan; add shiitakes. Cover and set aside for 20 minutes. Drain shiitakes; reserve milk. Mince mushrooms. Cook potatoes in a small saucepan until tender, but firm; set aside.

Wipe mushrooms clean with damp paper towel. Thinly slice 1/2 pound of the mushrooms, halve 1/4 pound and quarter remaining 1/4 pound mushrooms to yield three different mushroom shapes.

Heat butter in a heavy-bottomed 5-quart saucepan; add onion and garlic. Sauté over medium-high heat until onion turns translucent. Add flour, stirring to incorporate ingredients. Cook 1 to 2 minutes longer. Add wine, water, vegetarian powder, tomato juice, Worcestershire, reserved shiitake milk, salt and pepper; stir until well blended. Bring to a boil; add mushrooms, minced shiitakes and cooked potatoes. Simmer 5 to 10 minutes over medium heat until mushrooms are tender. Remove from heat; stir in sour cream, nutmeg and paprika. Serve over hot buttered egg noodles. May be refrigerated and reheated in a microwave or moderate 350-degree F oven. Keeps well in the refrigerator for 1 week.

*Available in Asian and Oriental markets.

Chapter 9

Desserts

New York Cheesecake

There is nothing that a dynamite slice of cheesecake cannot cure.
We have been witnesses to a baffling phenomenon of miraculous healing
time and time again at The Cheese Factory. One bite of this silky,
sweet, citrus-scented sensation and all concerns fade away.
Try it for yourself!

Yield: 1 cheesecake

12 to 16 servings

Crust:
1¼ cups graham cracker crumbs
¼ cup powdered sugar
⅓ cup butter, melted

Filling:
4 packages (8 ounces each)
 cream cheese
1¼ cups sugar
6 large eggs
1 cup sour cream
2 teaspoons vanilla extract
2 teaspoons orange zest

Put a springform pan together with bottom circle upside down so cake rests on a platform. (This facilitates unmolding cake at the end.) Line the base with a circle of waxed paper; line sides with a strip of waxed paper 4 inches high. Place pan on a large sheet of aluminum foil and tightly fold foil up and around bottom half of pan. (This prevents water from seeping into pan while cake bakes immersed in a water bath.)

Prepare water bath by filling a large baking pan with 1 inch hot water. Place pan into a 325-degree F oven.

Combine graham cracker crumbs, powdered sugar and butter in a small bowl. Press mixture onto bottom of pan. Place crust in freezer for 10 minutes.

Place cream cheese in bowl of electric mixer and mix on medium speed until softened, using paddle attachment. Add sugar, then eggs one at a time. Add sour cream, vanilla and orange zest. Scrape down sides of bowl and blend until mixture is smooth. Pour cheese mixture into prepared pan and gently place into water bath. Bake 1 hour at 325 degrees F for regular oven; 300 degrees F for convection oven. After baking, turn heat off and leave in oven 1 hour. Remove cake and place on wire rack. Chill overnight before serving.

Carrot Cake

Although carrots star in this production, it is the fragrant, juicy background flavors that shine in harmonious composure. Full of moist, fruity textures and infused with subtle, sweet spices, this homey baked treat loves its sugary coat of cream cheese frosting. Impressive yet easy to produce, novice cooks will find their efforts well rewarded in this dessert. (See photo on page 95)

Yield: 1 three-layer carrot cake

12 to 16 servings

3 cups flour
1³/₄ cups brown sugar
1³/₄ cups granulated sugar
1¹/₂ teaspoons ground cinnamon
¹/₄ teaspoon ground nutmeg
¹/₈ teaspoon ground cloves
2 teaspoons baking soda
2 teaspoons baking powder
¹/₂ teaspoon salt
2 cups shredded carrots
1¹/₂ cups vegetable oil
1 cup milk
2 teaspoons vanilla extract
4 ounces sour cream
¹/₂ cup canned crushed pineapple, drained
¹/₂ cup raisins
¹/₂ cup chopped walnuts
¹/₂ cup shredded sweetened coconut
4 eggs, beaten

Cream Cheese Frosting:
2 cups (4 sticks) butter, softened
1 package (12 ounces) cream cheese, softened
6 cups powdered sugar
¹/₈ teaspoon salt
2 tablespoons vanilla extract
1 teaspoon lemon juice
1 teaspoon almond extract
3 teaspoons orange zest

Preheat oven to 350 degrees F. Spray three springform pans or three 9¹/₂-inch round cake pans with non-stick cooking spray. Line bottoms with waxed paper circles and spray with additional cooking spray.

Combine flour, brown sugar, granulated sugar, cinnamon, nutmeg, cloves, baking soda, baking powder and salt in a large bowl; toss with carrots. In a separate bowl, combine oil, milk, vanilla, sour cream, pineapple, raisins, walnuts, coconut and eggs; mix well. Slowly add wet ingredients to dry; mix well to combine. Pour ¹/₃ mixture into each prepared pan and bake 20 to 25 minutes or until cake springs back when lightly touched with fingertips. Remove from oven and cool on wire rack.

To make frosting, cream butter and cream cheese in bowl of electric mixer using paddle attachment. Gradually add sugar until blended. Add salt, vanilla, lemon juice, almond extract, orange zest and blend until smooth.

Unmold cooled cakes and ice tops with frosting. Stack one on top of another to obtain 3 layers and finish by icing sides. Garnish with toasted coconut, a sprinkling of assorted dried fruit or thinly sliced pineapple, if desired.

Glorious Chocolate Cake

Those who succumb to this dessert lay claims to spiritual sojourns into a kingdom where Creation and chocolate are synonymous. Vibrantly flavored and velvety smooth, the moist texture and deep richness of this confection conspire to send one into a condition of ecstacy where visions of chocolaty fulfillment soothe the soul. (See photo on page 93)

Yield: 1 nine-inch layer cake

12 to 16 servings

Cake:
 1 package Devil's food cake mix
   (10$1/4$ ounces)

Mousse filling:
 2 packages (12 ounces each)
   semisweet chocolate chips
 1$2/3$ cups heavy cream
 2 egg yolks
 1/3 cup Crème de Cacao syrup,
   or 2 tablespoons coffee liqueur
 5 egg whites (room temperature)
 1/2 teaspoon cream of tartar
 1 cup sugar
 1/2 cup cold water

Chocolate decorations:
 1 cup semisweet chocolate chips
 2 tablespoons light corn syrup

Ganache:
 1/2 cup heavy cream
 6 tablespoons light corn syrup
 1 package (12 ounces) semisweet
   chocolate chips

To make cake, line two 9-inch springform pans with parchment paper and spray with nonstick cooking spray. Prepare and bake cake according to package directions. Remove from oven; cool 10 minutes in pans. Place on wire rack to cool completely.

To make mousse filling, place chocolate chips in a medium bowl. Heat 1 cup of the cream in a small saucepan just until boiling; pour over chocolate chips. Let sit for 2 minutes; stir with whisk until thoroughly blended. Cool; stir in egg yolks, one at a time. Add Crème de Cacao; stir to blend; set aside.

Beat egg whites with cream of tartar in bowl of electric mixer until stiff peaks form. Combine sugar and cold water in a small saucepan; stir constantly until mixture comes to a boil. Heat syrup until candy thermometer registers 240 degrees F. Drizzle hot candy syrup over beaten egg whites taking care to avoid wire whip attachment and sides of bowl. Whip on high speed until bowl feels cool. Slowly pour chocolate mixture into egg white mixture, beating on slow speed until completely mixed.

Whip remaining 2/3 cup cream in a small bowl until stiff peaks form. Fold into chocolate mousse until no white lumps are visible. Cover with plastic wrap and chill 2 hours in refrigerator until set.

To make chocolate decorations, melt chocolate chips in top of double boiler. Add corn syrup; stir to combine. Place a sheet of plastic wrap in a shallow microwavable tray. Allow chocolate mixture to cool a little, then pour into pan; cover tray tightly with plastic wrap and freeze overnight. Remove tray from freezer and microwave on defrost until chocolate softens (do not melt). Remove softened chocolate from tray and place between 2 sheets of parchment paper. Roll to a thickness of 1/8 inch. Return to freezer for 5 minutes until chocolate no longer shines. Cut shapes using cookie cutters. (We use heart, duck, star and angel cookie cutters at the restaurant.) Chill until ready to serve. (Decorations may be made a few days ahead and refrigerated.)

To assemble cake, slice off rounded tops of cooled layers with a serrated knife. Place first layer in springform pan and cover top evenly with about half of the mousse filling. (Reserve 1 cup filling for decorating cake.) Cover with second layer and spread remaining filling over top; freeze 24 hours.

To decorate, place frozen cake on wire rack over a cookie sheet. To make ganache, combine cream and corn syrup in a small saucepan; heat until mixture comes to a boil. Place chocolate chips in a small bowl; pour cream mixture over chips. Allow chocolate to melt 30 seconds; stir until smooth and lump-free. Stir ganache frequently to prevent skin from forming or place a damp cloth over bowl. (If ganache seems too thick, add additional warm cream. If too thin, add additional chocolate chips.)

Pour warm ganache over cake and return to freezer for 30 minutes. (Ideal pouring temperature of ganache is tepid to lukewarm. For a smoother finish, ganache may be poured over twice.) Fill a pastry bag, fitted with a #2 star tip with remaining mousse and pipe a ribbon of mousse around bottom edge of cake. Pipe top edge of cake with 8 to 12 mousse rosettes (spaced equally) and insert chocolate shapes. Freeze cake 30 minutes to set mousse. Remove cake from freezer and place in refrigerator 30 to 45 minutes before serving.

Hazelnut Torte

Hazelnuts or filberts, as they are sometimes referred to, belong to the birch family. Once covering northern Europe and now growing in the northwest United States, they have long been regarded by pastry makers as one of the supreme dessert nuts. As with all nuts, oven roasting is recommended to bring out their delicate characteristics and full nuttiness. Indulge your senses in a luxurious and elegant ending lost in a hazelnut haze, surrounded by chocolate cliffs layered with clouds of fresh whipped cream. What a way to go!

Yield: 1 four-layer cake

12 to 16 servings

Cake:
- 10 egg whites, room temperature
- 3/4 teaspoon salt
- 1 1/2 cups sugar
- 10 egg yolks, room temperature
- 2 teaspoons vanilla extract
- 1/2 cup toasted hazelnuts (page 12), ground
- 1/2 cup toasted pecans (page 12), ground
- 1/2 cup dry bread crumbs
- 1 1/2 teaspoons baking powder

Filling:
- 1 1/2 cups chilled heavy cream
- 2/3 cup sifted powdered sugar
- 1 teaspoon vanilla extract

Frosting:
- 1 package (6 ounces) semisweet chocolate chips (1 cup)
- 6 tablespoons (3/4 stick) unsalted butter
- 2 cups sifted powdered sugar
- 2 tablespoons instant coffee
- 1/4 cup hot water
- 1 1/2 teaspoons vanilla extract
- Whole hazelnuts for garnish

Preheat oven to 350 degrees F.

Spray bottom and sides of four springform or four 9-inch round cake pans with nonstick cooking spray. Line bottoms with parchment paper and spray paper.

To make cake, combine egg whites and 1/2 teaspoon of the salt in bowl of electric mixer; beat at medium speed until soft peaks form. Slowly beat in 3/4 cup of the sugar, 2 tablespoons at a time; continue to beat until soft peaks form. Transfer beaten egg whites to a clean bowl.

Beat egg yolks in bowl of electric mixer at medium speed until thick and lemon colored, about 5 minutes. Slowly beat in remaining 3/4 cup sugar and beat 5 minutes more; add vanilla.

In a small bowl, combine nuts, bread crumbs, baking powder and remaining 1/4 teaspoon salt; stir into yolk mixture using rubber spatula. Fold in beaten egg white mixture. Divide batter equally among prepared pans. Smooth tops with spatula and bake 25 minutes or until tops spring back when gently pressed. Remove pans from oven; immediately invert onto wire racks covered with waxed paper.

Cool to room temperature and remove parchment circles from cakes.

To make filling, whip cream in bowl of electric mixer until soft peaks form. Slowly add sugar and vanilla; refrigerate.

To make frosting, melt chocolate and butter in the top of a double boiler. Remove from heat and whisk in sugar. Dissolve coffee in hot water; whisk into chocolate mixture; add vanilla.

To assemble cake, place single cake layer on serving plate and spread top with 1/3 of the filling. Repeat with second and third layers. Top with fourth layer and spread frosting on sides and top of cake (reserve 1/2 cup for decoration). Place remaining frosting in pastry bag fitted with a #2 star tip; pipe swirls around top edge of cake. Garnish with whole toasted hazelnuts; refrigerate. Allow torte to sit at room temperature 15 minutes before serving.

Cloud 9

*A celestial endeavor featuring strips of dark chocolate
sponge cake, buried in an avalanche of white chocolate mousse.
Richly subtle and light as a feather, this revered delicacy is a
graceful ending to any meal. Celebrate a special occasion by
dazzling your guests with this devastatingly divine dessert.*
(See photo on page 96)

Yield: 8 servings

Cake:
   1 box (18.25 ounces) chocolate
       cake mix

White chocolate mousse:
   24 ounces Swiss white chocolate,
        coarsely chopped
   4 cups heavy cream

Raspberry sauce:
   2 cups raspberries, fresh or frozen,
       thawed
   1/3 cup sugar
   1/4 cup Chambord raspberry liqueur
   1 teaspoon lemon juice

White chocolate curls:
   12 ounces bulk white chocolate,
        about 3/4 inch thick

   Fresh raspberries for garnish

Prepare cake according to package directions and bake in a 9x13-inch pan; cool on wire rack. Cut and remove three 1x13-inch strips; set aside (there will be cake left over).

To make mousse, line a 10x14x2-inch baking pan with parchment or waxed paper; leave a 2-inch overhang on the ends. Place chocolate in an ovenproof dish and melt in a 150-degree F oven, about 15 to 20 minutes. In a chilled large bowl, whip cream until soft peaks form using an electric hand mixer on high speed. Rapidly pour warm chocolate over whipped cream; immediately fold mixtures together using a large wire whisk. Work quickly, but gently as mixture sets up rapidly; mix until just blended. (Do not overwhip mousse or it will become grainy.) Transfer mousse into prepared pan; spread evenly. Press reserved cake strips into mousse, burying them halfway down (see diagram). Smooth top with metal spatula. Place in refrigerator for 30 minutes or until surface has set. Cover pan with plastic wrap, then wrap tightly with foil. Refrigerate mousse for a minimum of 6 hours or overnight.

To make raspberry sauce, combine raspberries, sugar, liqueur and lemon juice in a food processor with metal blade. Process 30 to 45 seconds or until smooth. Strain through a fine-meshed sieve into a small bowl. Cover with plastic wrap and chill.

To make chocolate curls, place chocolate on a piece of waxed paper and soften in microwave on 50 percent power for 10-second intervals (the chocolate should soften slightly, but not melt.) Remove from microwave and wrap end of chocolate in plastic wrap so heat from your hand doesn't cause it to melt. Use a vegetable peeler to scrape 1 edge of chocolate in a downward motion, forming loose shavings. Allow chocolate curls to fall onto waxed paper; continue to make curls with remaining chocolate. Refrigerate until ready to use.

To assemble, remove cake from refrigerator and uncover. Invert onto a large, chilled serving platter. Peel paper from top of cake and trim sides to an even shape. Remove chocolate curls from refrigerator. Use a metal spatula to scoop up curls and place on top of cake. Keep refrigerated until ready to serve. To serve, place cake on dessert plates and spoon raspberry sauce around edge. Garnish with fresh raspberries, if desired.

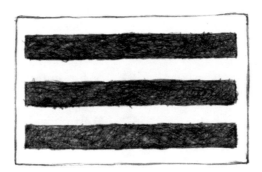

Note: Cake may be made a day ahead. Cut leftover cake into small squares and eat as a snack. For best results, we use Lindt Swiss White Chocolate.

Mocha Pecan Pie

*The pecan, a distant relative of the walnut, is native to North America.
Its name is Algonquin and its chief production is in the south central states.
Chocolate is made from the beans of the cacao tree, which grows only
within 20 degrees of the equator. The making of fine chocolate is an art
that depends on the careful selection and blending of beans
and even more careful roasting to bring out the flavors.
The alliance of these two elements in this rich and luxurious
dessert inspires sighs of deep satisfaction.*

Yield 1 nine-inch pie

12 to 16 servings

Pie pastry:
21/4 cups flour
　1/2 teaspoon salt
　6 tablespoons butter, chilled
　3 tablespoons vegetable shortening
　1/2 cup ice water

Filling:
　1 package (6 ounces) semisweet
　　chocolate chips (1 cup)
　3 tablespoons Kahlua
　3 large eggs, beaten
　1/2 cup firmly packed brown sugar
　1 cup light corn syrup
　2 teaspoons vanilla extract
　1/4 teaspoon salt
　1/2 cup (1 stick) butter, melted
11/4 cups toasted pecans (page 12),
　　coarsely chopped

Place flour and salt in a medium bowl. Working quickly, cut butter into thin slices and add to bowl along with shortening. Using fingertips, swiftly incorporate ingredients until mixture resembles coarse meal. Drizzle water over dough and form into a ball. (Do not knead dough—compact with hands.) Wrap in waxed paper and chill 1 hour in refrigerator. Roll dough to fit a 9-inch pie pan; leave enough of an overhang to crimp edges. Refrigerate or freeze until ready to use.

Preheat oven to 350 degrees F.

Melt chocolate with Kahlua in top of double boiler; set aside.

Combine eggs, sugar, corn syrup, vanilla and salt in bowl of an electric mixer. Beat 1 minute on medium speed until blended; add chocolate mixture; stir to blend. Stir in butter and 1 cup pecans. Pour mixture into unbaked pie shell and sprinkle remaining 1/4 cup pecans over top. Bake approximately 45 minutes or until barely set in center. (Pie will set as it cools.) Serve with whipped cream or ice cream and a great cup of coffee!

Chocolate Mousse with Raspberry Sauce

*One's initial encounter with the deep mystery of a dark chocolate mousse
is nothing short of a miracle. Contrary to some beliefs, producing
one of these satiny, smooth specimens does not require a high
degree of skill. Passionate anticipation of the first magical
mouthful is the only ingredient necessary to propel
any unseasoned cook into mousse mastery.*

Yield: 8 servings

2 packages (4 ounces each) semisweet chocolate, chopped
2 pints heavy cream
1 teaspoon vanilla extract
1/2 ounce Amaretto (optional)
1/2 cup powdered sugar
6 egg whites
1/2 cup slivered toasted almonds
(page 12)

Raspberry Sauce:
2 packages (16 ounces each)
frozen raspberries, thawed
1/2 cup sugar
1/8 teaspoon salt
1 tablespoon cornstarch
2 tablespoons cold water
1 tablespoon lemon juice
2 tablespoons Crème de Cassis
(optional)

Melt chocolate in top of a double boiler. Combine cream, vanilla, Amaretto and powdered sugar in bowl of electric mixer; whip until stiff peaks are formed. In a separate bowl, beat egg whites to stiff peaks. Slowly add whipped cream to warm chocolate using a wire whisk. Fold in beaten egg whites using a rubber spatula. Divide mousse evenly into 8 stemmed glasses or spoon into a large, decorative serving bowl. Chill until served.

To prepare sauce, purée raspberries in a blender; reserve 1 cup. Place puréed raspberries in a small saucepan. Add sugar and salt; cook over medium heat 2 to 3 minutes. Combine cornstarch with water and add to raspberry mixture. Bring to a boil and remove from heat; cool. Add lemon juice, liqueur and reserved 1 cup raspberries. To serve, spoon sauce on a dessert plate; place a serving of mousse over sauce and sprinkle with almonds.

Cheese Strudel with Pears

This elegant Austrian pastry does not require much baking expertise, making it a perfect candidate for rookies. Quick and easy to prepare, this light finale performs a lively dance upon the palate. For variation, choose from a bounty of fresh, canned or preserved fruits available at all supermarkets. If you have never worked with phyllo dough, be sure to read the instructions for handling on the package. The dough is paper thin and dries out quickly. Keep it covered with a damp cloth while you work. Do not be concerned if it cracks or breaks; it is very forgiving. Simply brush with melted butter, patch the pieces together and continue.

Yield: 2 strudels

12 servings

1 package (8 ounces) cream
    cheese
1/2 cup plus 2 tablespoons sugar
1 large egg
2 tablespoons sifted flour
1 tablespoon orange zest
1 carton (8 ounces)
    cottage cheese, drained
1 can (16 ounces) pears,
    drained and quartered
12 sheets phyllo dough
    (14x18 inches)
1 cup (2 sticks) unsalted butter,
    melted
4 tablespoons sliced toasted
    almonds (page 12), coarsely
    chopped
1 egg
1 teaspoon water
2 teaspoons powdered sugar

Preheat oven to 350 degrees F. Lightly butter a 9x13-inch baking sheet.

Soften cream cheese in bowl of electric mixer with paddle attachment. Add 1/2 cup of the sugar; beat until smooth and fluffy. Incorporate egg, then slowly mix in flour and orange zest. Fold in cottage cheese with a rubber scraper until well blended. (The curd will still be evident in mixture.)

Cover work area with waxed paper. Place 1 sheet phyllo dough on paper and lightly brush with butter; sprinkle with 1 teaspoon of the nuts. Place next 4 layers on top of first layer; brush each layer with butter and sprinkle with nuts. Butter last layer, but omit nuts (there should be a total of 6 layers).

Place half the cheese mixture and half the pears along the long side of the phyllo dough, leaving a 1-inch border on each end and side. Start to roll from edge containing filling. Once filling is enclosed, fold in sides and continue rolling to the end; brush along entire strudel with butter. Repeat process for second strudel.

Using a wide metal spatula, transfer strudels to a buttered cookie sheet, seam side down. Prepare egg wash by slightly beating egg; add water and brush over each strudel. Gently make 4 slits on top with a sharp paring knife. Sprinkle each strudel with 1 tablespoon sugar. Bake 30 minutes or until golden brown. Cool slightly on baking sheet and dust with powdered sugar. Serve plain or with whipped cream.

Creola's Flan

A rich, smooth, vanilla-scented custard is compliments of the former nanny of one of our cooks. Easy to make in advance, this recipe holds its own among the vast repertoire of continuously evolving desserts presented at the restaurant. It is not uncommon to find the bakery case surrounded by guests attempting to make a selection from the abundant treasury of sumptuous delights.

Yield: 8 flans

1¹/2 cups plus ¹/3 cup sugar
¹/2 cup hot water
 4 large eggs
 4 egg yolks
¹/3 cup sugar
¹/8 teaspoon salt
 1 cup heavy cream
2¹/2 cups milk
 2 teaspoons vanilla extract
   Ground nutmeg (optional)

Cook 1¹/2 cups of the sugar in a heavy-bottomed 2-quart saucepan over low heat, stirring until caramelized or amber colored. Slowly add hot water, stirring vigorously until smooth.

Using 8 individual custard cups, pour equal amounts caramel sauce into each cup and set aside.

Beat together in a bowl until blended, but not foamy: eggs, egg yolks, remaining ¹/3 cup sugar and salt. In a medium saucepan, combine cream and milk; scald over medium-high heat. Slowly add hot milk to egg mixture, whisking continuously, taking care not to scramble eggs. Add vanilla and stir.

Preheat oven to 325 degrees F. Prepare a water bath by filling an 18x12-inch pan with 1 inch boiling water. Pour custard mixture equally over caramel sauce in cups and sprinkle with nutmeg. Set cups in water bath and bake 45 minutes or until tops are mildly glazed and a wooden pick inserted in center ensures custard is firm. Remove baked cups and discard hot water. Fill pan with 1 inch cold water and return baked cups to cool. Place in refrigerator to chill. To serve, unmold by running a thin paring knife around edge of custard and inverting onto serving dish.

Note: The recipe can be made in larger amounts and stored in the refrigerator for 5 days.

Tazmanian Toffee Crunch

*A crunchy candy creation bestowed upon us by an
Australian staff member, this down under delight is too easy
to make and too good to be true. For variation, pour the
toffee mixture over whole toasted almonds, cashews,
hazelnuts or pecans and eliminate the chocolate.
This recipe makes a fine gift nestled in a decorative tin.*

Yield: 1 3/4 pounds

1 cup (2 sticks) butter
1 cup sugar
2/3 cup semisweet chocolate chips
1 package (8 ounces) sliced
   toasted almonds (page 12),
   coarsely chopped

Line an 8x8-inch pan with aluminum foil. Melt butter in a heavy-bottomed 1-quart saucepan over medium heat. Add sugar and cook approximately 10 minutes, stirring constantly until color turns to a creamy light tan. (Be careful not to burn.) Test by dropping small amount into a cup of cold water. It should curl and harden when ready. Stir in 1/3 cup of the nuts. Pour into a foil-lined pan and distribute evenly; cool.

Melt half of the chocolate in the top of a small double boiler. Spread melted chocolate over cooled toffee mixture and sprinkle with half the remaining nuts. Allow chocolate to set at room temperature several hours or until completely hardened. Invert candy onto another 8x8-inch pan and repeat procedure for the reverse side: melt remaining half of chocolate in double boiler; spread over toffee and sprinkle with remaining nuts. Allow chocolate to harden. To serve, break candy into uneven, jagged shapes.

Divinity

*A white fudge candy made of whipped egg whites, sugar and nuts,
this recipe is simple to prepare, but requires infinite patience and careful
temperature control to achieve full promise. A perfect holiday project, these
precious morsels will add pure sweetness and delight to any festive gathering.*

Yield: 30 to 35 pieces

   2 egg whites, room temperature
2 1/2 cups sugar
 1/2 cup light corn syrup
 1/2 cup water
 1/4 teaspoon salt
   1 tablespoon vanilla extract
 1/2 cup chopped nuts

In large bowl of electric mixer, beat egg whites until stiff, but not dry.

Combine sugar, corn syrup, water and salt in a heavy-bottomed 3-quart saucepan. Cook over medium heat until syrup comes to a boil. Remove from heat. Cover pan and let sit 2 minutes to melt sugar from sides of pan. Remove cover and place candy thermometer in pan. Return to heat until temperature reaches 250 degrees. Remove from heat and gradually pour half the syrup in a steady stream into beaten egg whites with mixer on slow speed. Increase speed to medium and mix until well blended. Return pan to heat until temperature on thermometer reaches 270 degrees. Remove from heat and slowly add remaining half of syrup in a steady stream while beating at medium speed. Beat until candy loses some of its gloss and soft peaks form, about 10 to 15 minutes.

Line a cookie sheet with waxed paper. Stir vanilla and nuts into mixture and drop by spoonfuls onto cookie sheet. Cool and store at room temperature in an airtight container. (Do not refrigerate.)

Caribbean Chocolate Bananas

A charming way to treat a banana, this tantalizing tropical fruit provides excellent snack satisfaction for all ages. The chocolate sauce itself may be drizzled warm over angel food cake or dessert crêpes filled with ice cream. Pour it into plastic ice cube trays, bury a whole roasted almond or hazelnut in each compartment and freeze. Dip fresh strawberries or shortbread cookies in the sauce for enhanced flavor fulfillment.

Yield: 8 chocolate-coated bananas

4 ripe bananas
8 Popsicle sticks
1/2 cup toasted chopped nuts
    (page 12)
1 cup (2 sticks) butter
1 can (15 ounces) coconut cream*
2 bags (12 ounces each) semisweet
    chocolate chips

Peel bananas and cut in half horizontally. Insert a Popsicle stick into each half, place in sealed storage container and freeze.

Melt butter in a medium saucepan over low heat. Add coconut cream, chocolate chips and stir continuously until chocolate is melted. Remove from heat and allow to cool 10 minutes.

Pour chocolate mixture into a small bowl and dip frozen bananas, one at a time. Roll dipped bananas in nuts and serve immediately or freeze until ready to use.

Note: Choose macadamias, almonds, peanuts or a combination of nuts.

*Available in liquor department of supermarkets.

Broiled Fresh Pineapple

Pineapple is a tropical fruit available almost all year with peak season between March and June. When selecting this relative of Spanish moss, keep in mind that pineapples do not ripen after picking; their color is not a reliable indication of ripeness. Judge them by scent, weight and softness. Choose large pineapples, which will have proportionately less shell and core. Enjoy this succulent, refreshing dessert as is or with whipped cream, ice cream, sorbet, frozen yogurt or crème anglaise.

Yield: 16 slices

2 large ripe pineapples
    (3 3/4 pounds each)
1 cup apple juice
1 cup sugar
1 teaspoon ground cinnamon
1/2 teaspoon ground cloves
    Strawberries or seasonal fruit of
    choice (optional)

Using a sharp knife, cut both ends off pineapples; reserve tops.

Stand fruit up on work surface and slice off shell. Start at the top, working downward, rotating fruit until all the shell is removed. Lay pineapple down and cut in half vertically. Cut each half in half again to obtain 4 even slices, approximately 1/2 inch thick.

Using an apple corer, the back of a pastry tip or tiny cookie cutter, remove center core in each slice. Place pineapple rings in a shallow baking pan and add apple juice.

Combine sugar, cinnamon and cloves in a small bowl; sprinkle half the mixture over pineapple. Broil 3 to 5 minutes or until golden brown. Turn slices over, sprinkle with remaining sugar mixture and return to broiler for an additional 3 to 5 minutes or until golden.

Place reserved pineapple tops in center of an oval serving platter and arrange slices around tops, overlapping slightly. Pour pan juices over pineapple and garnish with fresh strawberries or any preferred seasonal fruit.

Note: Each pineapple should yield 8 rings.

Poached Pears in Burgundy Wine

Originating approximately 4000 years ago somewhere between central Europe and northeastern Asia, pears became a prized fruit of the wealthy elite and a particular favorite of the French nobility. There are now an estimated 2000 to 5000 varieties, the most common being the Bartlett, a summer pear. This recipe calls for the Bosc, a winter pear on the market from October through May. The Bosc has very good flavor and an elegant shape which it retains in cooking, making it especially suited to poaching. Steeped in the perfumed essence of spiced, hearty Burgundy, these pears can be served with savory dishes to bring out contrasting flavors. (See photo on page 94)

Yield: 8 pears

4 quarts Burgundy wine
2 cups sugar
12 whole cloves
6 cinnamon sticks
    (4 inches long)
12 fresh green peppercorns*
1 piece fresh gingerroot,
    (2 inches long) peeled and
    quartered
    Peel of 1 lemon
8 large Bosc pears or any firm
    variety available, with stems
    intact

Fill a 6-quart stainless or porcelain pot with Burgundy. Add sugar and stir to dissolve. Add cloves, cinnamon sticks, peppercorns and gingerroot. Remove yellow lemon peel with a paring knife, taking care to avoid bitter white pith; add to pot. Using a vegetable peeler, remove skins from pears, taking care to preserve smooth outer surface (as if sculpted). Keep stems intact.

As each pear is peeled, immerse into wine mixture. When all pears are peeled, place pot over high heat and bring to a boil. Reduce heat and simmer partially covered, approximately 45 minutes or until pears are tender, but firm. Remove from heat; cool and chill overnight before serving. Pears will keep refrigerated when stored in wine for 2 weeks. To serve, float pears in spiced Burgundy.

*Available in specialty food section of supermarkets.

No-Fat and Low-Fat Guidelines

No-Fat and Low-Fat Guidelines

Maximize flavor—minimize fat. Enlist the support of these excellent flavoring tips in a daily reduced fat repertoire.

Fruit juices, citrus juices and zest, flavored vinegar, vegetarian flavor-enhanced soup powders, herbs and spices, fat-free condiments and sauces, such as barbecue sauce, marinara sauce, mustard and salsas, are great flavor enhancers.

◆

For soups, sauces, stews and stir-frys: use juices, vinegars or vegetable broths in place of or combined with reduced amounts of oil.

◆

To marinate fresh vegetables or dress crisp leafy greens: use small amounts of highly flavored oils, such as extra-virgin olive oil, dark sesame oil and walnut or hazelnut oil.

◆

Fresh herbs and spices and fat-free condiments are ideal flavor boosters on pastas, grains, potatoes and vegetables.

◆

Low-fat or no-fat mayonnaise is a perfect substitute for creamy based salad dressings.

◆

Thickening skim milk with a little cornstarch and adding fresh herbs is a good white sauce base from which to improvise.

◆

Roasting, charbroiling and grilling are great cooking techniques that extract concentrated flavors from foods without the use of excessive seasonings or fat.

Conversions, Equivalents and Standards

Weights and Measures Conversions*

WEIGHT MEASURES CONVERSIONS

U.S.	Metric
1/4 ounce	8 grams
1/2 ounce	15 grams
1 ounce	30 grams
4 ounces	115 grams
8 ounces (1/2 pound)	225 grams
16 ounces (1 pound)	450 grams
32 ounces (2 pounds)	900 grams
40 ounces (2 1/2 pounds)	1 kilogram

VOLUME MEASURES CONVERSIONS

U.S.	Metric
1 teaspoon	5 milliliters
1 tablespoon	15 milliliters
1 fluid ounce (2 tablespoons)	30 milliliters
2 fluid ounces (1/4 cup)	60 milliliters
8 fluid ounces (1 cup)	240 milliliters
16 fluid ounces (1 pint)	480 milliliters
32 fluid ounces (1 quart)	950 milliliters (.95 liter)
128 fluid ounces (1 gallon)	3.75 liters

*metric amounts are nearest equivalents

Weights and Measures Equivalencies

Dash	less than $1/8$ teaspoon
3 teaspoons	1 tablespoon ($1/2$ fluid ounce)
2 tablespoons	$1/8$ cup (1 fluid ounce)
4 tablespoons	$1/4$ cup (2 fluid ounces)
$5^{1}/3$ tablespoons	$1/3$ cup ($2^{2}/3$ fluid ounces)
8 tablespoons	$1/2$ cup (4 fluid ounces)
$10^{2}/3$ tablespoons	$2/3$ cup ($5^{1}/3$ fluid ounces)
12 tablespoons	$3/4$ cup (6 fluid ounces)
14 tablespoons	$7/8$ cup (7 fluid ounces)
16 tablespoons	1 cup (8 fluid ounces)
1 jigger	$1^{1}/2$ ounces (3 tablespoons)
1 gill	$1/2$ cup
1 cup	8 fluid ounces (240 milliliters)
2 cups	1 pint (480 milliliters)
2 pints	1 quart (approximately 1 liter)
4 quarts	1 gallon (3.75 liters)
8 quarts	1 peck
4 pecks	1 bushel
1 ounce	28.35 grams (rounded to 30)
16 ounces	1 pound (453.59 grams rounded to 450)
1 kilogram	2.2 pounds

Standards

LIQUID STANDARDS

1 milliliter=0.035 fluid ounces
1 fluid ounce=30 milliliters
1 US pint=16 fluid ounces
1UK pint=20 fluid ounces
500 milliliters=16 fluid ounces=2 cups
1 liter=1 quart

SOLID WEIGHT STANDARDS

1 gram=0.35 ounces
1 ounce=30 grams

LENGTH CONVERSIONS

1 centimeter=0.394 inch
1 inch=2.54 centimeters

Temperature Conversions

Degrees Fahrenheit (°F.)	Degrees Celsius (°C.)
32	0
40	4
140	60
150	65
160	70
170	75
212	100
275	135
300	150
325	165
350	175
375	190
400	205
425	220
450	230
475	245
500	260

Glossary

Glossary

Asian rice: (Jasmine rice) A fragrant, quick-cooking white rice from Thailand. Available in Asian markets.

Balsamic vinegar: An aged Italian vinegar with a dark, mellow, subtle flavor.

Calrose rice: A glutenous, sticky rice; great for nori rolls. Available in Asian markets.

Chipotle peppers: Dried, smoked jalapeño peppers. Available in most supermarkets and Hispanic markets.

Chipotle peppers in adobo sauce: Dry, smoked jalapeño peppers in a spicy tomato sauce. Available in Hispanic markets.

Cream of coconut: Stronger flavored and sweeter than coconut milk. Available in your grocer's liquor section.

Galanga: A close relative of ginger, this root is sold fresh, frozen and powdered. Available in Asian markets.

Hickory smoke: A liquid seasoning made from distilled smoke.

Hoisin sauce: A sweet and spicy Chinese sauce made of soy beans, garlic, chili peppers and spices.

Jicama: A crisp, crunchy, large root vegetable with white flesh. Very similar to a large water chestnut with a taste between an apple and a pear. Available in large supermarkets or Hispanic markets.

Lime leaves: Leaves from the lime tree used in Thai and Laotian cooking. Best if fresh, but dried are always available in Asian markets.

Nori: Sheets of dried seaweed which are used as a wrapper for rice and vegetables in nori rolls or crumbled in Japanese soups. Available in Asian markets.

Nori mat:	A bamboo mat used to make nori rolls. Available in Asian markets.
Phyllo:	Paper-thin sheets of flaky pastry dough.
Pimientos:	Canned, cooked red peppers.
Red curry paste:	A very hot paste of peppers and spices used in Thai cooking. Available in Asian markets and some supermarkets.
Rice wrapper:	A dry rice paper used in the making of Thai Spring Rolls. Available in Asian markets and some supermarkets.
Shiitake mushrooms:	Originally grown in Japanese oak forests, the spores have now been imported into the United States and home-grown. Fresh shiitake and dehydrated mushrooms are renowned for their intense flavor. Available in most supermarkets.
Star anise:	The star-shaped pod of a Chinese evergreen which has a slightly licorice flavor. Available in Asian markets.
Tahini:	A smooth paste made from ground sesame seeds.
Tamari:	A sugar-free, naturally brewed, wheat-free soy sauce.
Tamarind pods:	The dried seed pods from a small tropical tree and the base flavor of Worcestershire sauce; tart and distinctive. Available in Asian markets.
Tangerine peels:	The very flavorful dehydrated peel of tangerines. Available in Asian markets.
Wasabi:	Japanese horseradish that is usually sold as a powder or a paste. Available in Asian markets.
Wood ear mushrooms:	Dehydrated mushrooms that, when reconstituted, expand to several times their size. These are used in Chinese dishes and are available in Asian markets.
Zest:	The outer colored part of the rind of citrus fruits.

Bibliography
&
Index

Bibliography

Collin, Annemarie. *The Natural Gourmet.* Ballantine Books, 1989.

The Editors of Time-Life Books. *Dried Beans & Grains.* Time-Life Books, 1982.

Rosso, Julie and Sheila Lukins. *The Silver Palate Cookbook.*
    Workman Publishing Co., 1982.

Rubash, Joyce. *The Master Dictionary of Food & Wine.* New York:
    International Thomson Publishing Inc., 1996.

Sahni, Julie. *Classic Indian Vegetarian & Grain Cooking.*
    William Morrow & Co., 1985.

Santa Maria, Jack. *Greek Vegetarian Cookery.* Shambhala Publications, 1984.

Shere, Lindsey Remolif. *Chez Parisse.* Random House, 1985.

Shurtleff, William and Akiko Aoyagi. *The Book of Tofu.* Ballantine Books, 1989.

Somerville, Annie. *Fields of Greens.* Bantam Books, 1993.

Index

A

B

C

A Love Affair with The Cheese Factory

The vision of a sparkling, animated restaurant, showcasing vegetarian international cuisine, gave birth to the restoration and conversion of an old cheese factory located in the heart of the Wisconsin Dells.

Old favorites served with a smile.

Our kitchen gardens.

Visit our old-fashioned soda fountain.

"It's the only place to eat between Chicago and Minnesota."

❖

"The first stop for anyone interested in getting beyond the pizza/burger/fries repertoire should be The Cheese Factory, Wisconsin Dells."

Chicago Tribune

❖

"Best breakfast on the North American continent!"

*Richard and Gail
Historic Bennett House Bed & Breakfast
Wisconsin Dells, Wisconsin*

❖

"I offer my congratulations on your excellence."

❖

"A slice of heaven."

The Dells/Delton Daily

❖

"The attire of the wait staff just adds more to the beautiful atmosphere, most excellent food, ambiance and people. I didn't want it to end."

❖

"Absolutely fantastic."

❖

"In recognition of Wisconsin's distinction as America's dairy state, The Cheese Factory Restaurant serves International Vegetarian Cuisine…"

Ladies Home Journal

"We sincerely appreciate your hospitality...the food was delicious and the service outstanding as always."

Wisconsin Dells
Visitor and Convention Bureau

◆

"The Cheese Factory features succulent dishes made from Wisconsin's acclaimed cheeses as well as other savory creations."

Better Homes and Gardens

◆

"Thank you again for making my birthday so special. I will never forget your kindness."

◆

"We have driven all over Wisconsin looking for something fun to do. We should have started here."

◆

"I am a vegetarian and surely surprised to find I could eat everything on your menu. God bless you…"

◆

"Excellent food, tastefully served; lovely, personable staff."

◆

"An atmosphere filled with employees that love their job, work together in harmony and treat their customers with kindness and the greatest respect that I've ever seen in any restaurant throughout the world!"

Tony and Jennifer
John's Pizzeria Ristorante—Chicago

◆

"Smiling isn't hard; just say Cheese Factory."

Milwaukee Journal Sentinel

◆

"Great vegetarian dishes without the sacrifice of flavor."

Paul Short, Executive Chef
Sandhill Inn
Merrimac, Wisconsin

Every occasion is special!

Music and dancing nightly in the San Francisco "Bridge" Lounge.

Cooking school classes are offered by the chefs of The Cheese Factory Restaurant.